소주
so ju
soju

고추장
gochujang
hot pepper paste

보자기
bojagi
gift wrapping cloth

반찬
banchan
side dishes

한복
hanbok
traditional
Korean dress

불고기
bulgogi
marinated
grilled meat

고속열차
go sok yeol cha
high speed train

KOREAN PICTURE DICTIONARY

LEARN 1,500 KOREAN WORDS AND PHRASES

Tina Cho
Korean text by Jaekeun Cho

TUTTLE Publishing

Tokyo | Rutland, Vermont | Singapore

Contents

A Basic Introduction to the Korean Language

This illustrated dictionary presents 1,500 frequently-used Korean words and phrases, including those that students need to know to pass the TOPIK, Test of Proficiency in Korean exam for non-native speakers. The dictionary is organized into 38 themes, each of which presents 30-40 words. Each section also has three to five sentences demonstrating the usage of the words. The words and sentences in the dictionary all appear in the following order: Hangeul characters, followed by the pronunciation in standard romanization form, followed by the English meaning.

History of the Korean Language

Researchers and linguists debate the origin of the Korean language. Some link it with the Altaic language family, which includes Mongolian, Turkic, and Tungusic language groups. The people within these groups lived in the Altai Mountain Region, which included northeastern Siberia to the Persian Gulf and from the Baltic Sea to China. These languages have similar components. The syllables are composed of a consonant + a vowel. They have vowel harmony. There are constraints on which vowels can be put together. And there are few consonant clusters.

Korean is one of the oldest spoken languages. History shows that two languages were spoken in Manchuria and on the Korean peninsula, the Northern or Puyo group and the Southern or Han group. During the 7th century, during the time of the Three Kingdoms Period, the Silla dialect became the dominant language. Then in the 10th century, the Koryo Dynasty moved the capital to Kaesong, in which the Kaesong dialect became the dominant language. At the end of the 14th century, the Chosun Dynasty moved the capital to Seoul; however, the language remained the same.

Before the 15th century, the Korean language was written using classical Chinese *hanja* characters that only elite scholarly people knew. This form of writing was too difficult to teach to all the people. Also, hanja reflected the meaning of words but not the sounds of the Korean language. The people couldn't express themselves properly in their language and had to simplify by using the Chinese *hanja*. Therefore, in 1443, King Sejong, with the help of scholars and his older children, created Hangeul, the phonetic Korean writing system. Hangeul became an easy writing system for the common people of Korea and has led to their high literacy rate. Hangeul tied the socio-economic classes of Korea together. Now, everyone could read and write, not just the literati. Hanja or Chinese characters are still used on formal documents and birth certificates as most Korean names and their meanings are derived from Chinese characters. Around 1800 *hanja* are still taught in Korean public schools.

Hangeul, noted as a scientific alphabet, has unified the country and has been their source of pride. During Japanese colonial occupation (1910–1945), Koreans were denied their language. They were forced to learn Japanese. But the people showed unity and resisted Japanese rule through their language. Just like other languages, there are dialects among the provinces, but the only dialect that is quite different is the dialect spoken on Jeju Island, south of the mainland. Today Koreans celebrate their language on October 9, Hangeul Day, and they are the only country in the world to do so.

The Korean Alphabet

The Korean alphabet was written specifically for the Korean language. Therefore, all Korean letters only make one or at the most two sounds; whereas, an English vowel can make several sounds. Hangeul is hard to use with foreign words. For example, when a word ends with a hard consonant, Koreans add an additional "eu" sound to the ending. Also, there is no f, v, or z in Hangeul. *Fork* is pronounced "po-keu." *Page* is pronounced "pay-jee," and *trump* is "trum-peu."

Hangeul is written in syllables rather than one letter behind the other. The shapes of the letters correspond to the shape of the mouth, tongue, and throat when pronouncing the sound. There are 10 vowels and 14 consonants. However, there are also 5 double consonants and 11 vowel combinations or dipthongs, which you'll see in the table below.

The Romanization of Korean

When writing Korean sounds using English letters, one must remember that the romanization will always make the same sound, unlike English vowels where an "a" can have many sounds like in bat, father, and date. You might see a Korean word written with romanization in various ways (for example: the city of Pyeongtaek, Pyongtaek, and Pyungtaek). Which way is correct? The Korean government has devised an official romanization system, but you might still see variations on signs and other places because of dialects and long ago there were different systems of spelling using romanization. Today there are two systems of spellings remaining: the McCune-Reischauer system and the government sponsored system. The first was devised in the early 1930s by children of missionaries who grew up in Asia, George M. McCune and Edwin O. Reischauer. It was used until 2000, when the government created its own Revised Romanization of Korean by the Ministry of Culture and Tourism. The government system is the official system and more commonly used. Below are examples of Korean romanization.

The Korean Alphabet and Roman Letters

Consonants

(1) Simple consonants

ㄱ	g, k	ㄴ	n	ㄷ	d, t	ㄹ	r, l	ㅁ	m
ㅂ	b, p	ㅅ	s	ㅇ	ng	ㅈ	j	ㅊ	ch
ㅋ	k	ㅌ	t	ㅍ	p	ㅎ	h		

(2) Double consonants

ㄲ	kk	ㄸ	tt	ㅃ	pp	ㅆ	ss	ㅉ	jj

Vowels

(1) Simple vowels

ㅏ	a	ㅓ	eo	ㅗ	o	ㅜ	u	ㅡ	eu
ㅣ	i	ㅐ	ae	ㅔ	e	ㅚ	oe	ㅟ	wi

(2) Compound vowels

ㅑ	ya	ㅕ	yeo	ㅛ	yo	ㅠ	yu	ㅒ	yae
ㅖ	ye	ㅘ	wa	ㅙ	wae	ㅝ	wo	ㅞ	we
ㅢ	ui								

5

Vowels

eo, **eu**, **ae** and **oe** are single vowels in romanized Korean as shown below. Therefore careful attention should be given to these vowels: take care that you are not splitting them into two. Also, careful attention should be given to "**u**/우"—do not read it as an English "you." Some common vowels which might confuse you could be:

a	아	<u>a</u>h, f<u>a</u>ther	(shorter than these *a*s)
eo	어	b<u>i</u>rd, s<u>e</u>rve	
o	오	b<u>a</u>ll, p<u>o</u>re	(shorter than this *a* or *o*)
u	우	b<u>oo</u>k, sch<u>oo</u>l	(shorter that these *oo*s)
eu	으	brok<u>e</u>n, gold<u>e</u>n	
i	이	b<u>ee</u>, sh<u>ee</u>p	(shorter than these *ee*s)
ae	애	<u>a</u>pple, b<u>a</u>d	
e	에	b<u>e</u>d, <u>e</u>gg	
oe	외	<u>wea</u>r, <u>we</u>lcome	

Consonants

You won't have much trouble pronouncing romanized Korean consonants except for some tensed ones which require a relatively strong muscular effort in the vocal organs without the expulsion of air. Here are some examples:

kk	ㄲ	s<u>k</u>i, s<u>k</u>y	(*k* after *s*)
tt	ㄸ	s<u>t</u>eak, s<u>t</u>ing	(*t* after *s*)
pp	ㅃ	s<u>p</u>eak, s<u>p</u>y	(*p* after *s*)
ss	ㅆ	<u>s</u>ea, <u>s</u>ir	(*s* before a vowel)
jj	ㅉ	bri<u>dg</u>e, mi<u>dg</u>et	(similar to a tutting sound in an exhaling way)

When reading in Hangeul, remember to read from top to bottom, then left to right. A consonant-vowel-consonant (CVC) syllable is written like this in Korean:

CV
C

If I was writing the word *bat* the Korean way, it would look like this: ba
t

The word *wonderful* would be grouped like this: wo de fu
n   r   l

Here's how the word *potato* looks in Korean: 감자
kam ja

Can you figure out this word? 학교
This is the word **hak/kyo**, meaning *school*.
Let's try the sentence, "I want a dog." How would you read this?

나는 개가 필요해.
Naneun gaega pilyohae.

This literally translates to "I dog want." Korean doesn't have the articles "a" or "an."

Grammar

The goal of this book is to teach vocabulary and phrases in Korean, allowing students to learn Korean grammar through induction. That is, students see how the grammar is used in context for communication, and draw conclusions as to grammar rules from these observations. Having said that, here are a few quick notes on Korean grammar to get you oriented.

In reading sentences, remember the verb is always last.

Subject, object, verb

EXAMPLE: In English we would say *Anna eats cake.*
            But in Korean, we would say *Anna cake eats.*

The other words in a sentence usually have topic markers. That means the words are marked as to whether they are the subject or object of the sentence.

EXAMPLE: In English: *Anna eats cake.* (subject, verb, object)
            In Korean: *Anna[ga] cake[ul] eats.*

Korean is not a tonal language like Chinese. But similarly, with English, when you ask a question, you have a rising tone toward the end. Declarative sentences end with a falling tone.

How to Use This Picture Dictionary

First, when learning Korean, it is best to play to your strengths. Focus on what you do best (for example, speaking or reading), and come back and learn the rest later.

Second, as the vocabulary in this book is arranged by theme, it is best to approach this dictionary topically, rather than systematically. Find the topics that are useful or of interest to you, and learn those words first. Third, practice and use the words in context with the conversations and phrases provided.

Fourth, listen to the audio recordings several times and read or say the Korean words aloud as you look at the pictures. You can also use your finger to trace out the corresponding Korean characters as you do so. If you have time, practice writing the characters in a notebook or on blank sheets of paper. This will help reinforce your memory of the vocabulary and phrases.

Finally, this picture dictionary should be just a beginning and not an end. If you find a topic that interest you, use the information in the picture dictionary as a jumping off point to learn more about that topic in Korean.

There are indexes at the end of the book which will help you find the meanings of words you have learned, but which you may have forgotten. The following information is included for each entry—the English word, the Korean word in Hangeul, the romanization, the lesson number and the order in which the word appeared in that lesson, followed by the page number where the word appears. For example:

English word	Hangeul	Romanization	Lesson and order	Page in book
a brief moment	짧은 순간	**jjalbeun sungan**	[15-30]	37

The free online audio contains recording of native Korean speakers reading all the vocabulary and sentences, so students can quickly acquire the correct pronunciation. A link to download the recordings can be found on page 96.

만나서 매우 반갑습니다!
Mannaseo maewoo bangapseupnida!

Nice to Meet You!

1

1 안녕하세요. 어떻게 지내세요?
An nyeong ha sae yo. Eotteokae jinaeseyo?
Hello, how are you?

2 잘 지냅니다. 감사합니다.
Jal jinap nida. Gamsa hapnida.
I am fine, thank you!

8 뭐요?
meo yo?
what?

9 만족
man jok
satisfied

3 만나다
man nada
to meet

10 행복
haengbok
happy

11 즐거운
jeul geo un
joyful

4 이씨가 김씨를 만나다.
Lee ciga Kim cireul man nada.
Mr. Lee, meet Ms. Kim.

5 안녕하세요.
An nyeong ha sae yo.
Hello !

6 만나서 반갑습니다.
Mannaseo bangapsseumnida.
Pleased to meet you!

7 소개하다
so gae hada
to introduce

12 부르다/불리다
bureuda/bullida
to call; to be called

13 친구
chin gu
friend

15 안녕하세요. 제이름은 스미스입니다.
Annyeonghasaeyo. Jeireumeun seumiseu ipnida.
이름이 뭐에요?
Ireumi meoeyo?
Hi, my name is Smith. What's your name?

16 제성은 홍이고, 이름은 길동입니다.
Jeseongeun Hongigo, ireumeun Gildong ipnida.
여기 명함있습니다.
Yeogi myongham itseumnida.
My surname is Hong, first name Gildong. Here's my namecard.

14 자신을 소개하다
jasineul sogaehada
introduce yourself

17 안녕! 나중에 봐!
Annyeong! Najoonge bwo!
Goodbye! See you!

18 조심해요!
Joshimhaeyo!
Take care!

Additional Vocabulary

23 이름
i reum
name

24 성
seong
surname

25 당신
dang shin
you (polite)

26 알다
al da
to know

27 국적
kuk jeok
nationality

28 악수
ak soo
shake hands

29 안다
an da
to hug

30 뽀뽀하다
ppo ppo hada
to kiss

31 미소
mi so
smile

32 흔들다
heun deul da
to wave

33 인사하다
in sa hada
to bow

34 환영하다
hwan yong hada
to welcome

35 대화를
daehwareul
시작하다
sijakhada
to start a
conversation

36 여보세요
yeobo seyo
hello (on the
phone)

37 표현하다
pyohyunhada
to express
(good wishes)

19 모임
mo im
gathering; meeting

20 손님
son nim
guest; customer

21 감사합니다
Gamsahapnida
Thank you!

22 천만에요.
Cheonman eyo.
You're welcome.

9

나의 가족

Na ui ga jok

2 My Family

Additional Vocabulary

23 아내 a nae wife	**31** 아기 a gi baby
24 남편 nam pyeon husband	**32** 큰아들 keun a deul older son
25 고모 go mo aunt (father's sister)	**33** 큰딸 keun ddal older daughter
26 삼촌 sam chon uncle	**34** 작은아들 jakeun a deul younger son
27 손자 son ja grandson	**35** 작은딸 jakeun ddal younger daughter
28 조카 jo ka cousin	**36** 막내 mak nae youngest
29 사촌 sa chon cousins	**37** 아빠 a ppa dad
30 가족 ga jok family	**38** 엄마 um ma mom

1 아들
a deul
son

2 남자
nam ja
male

3 여자
yeo ja
female

5 딸
ddal
daughter

4 아이들
a i deul
children

6 부모님
bu mo nim
parents

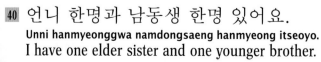

39 형제 자매가 몇명 있어요?
Hyungje jamaega myeotmyeong itseoyo?
How many brothers and sisters do you have?

40 언니 한명과 남동생 한명 있어요.
Unni hanmyeonggwa namdongsaeng hanmyeong itseoyo.
I have one elder sister and one younger brother.

7 할아버지
hal abuh ji
paternal grandfather

8 할머니
hal muh ni
paternal grandmother

9 외할아버지
oe hal abuh ji
maternal grandfather

10 외할머니
oe hal muh ni
maternal grandmother

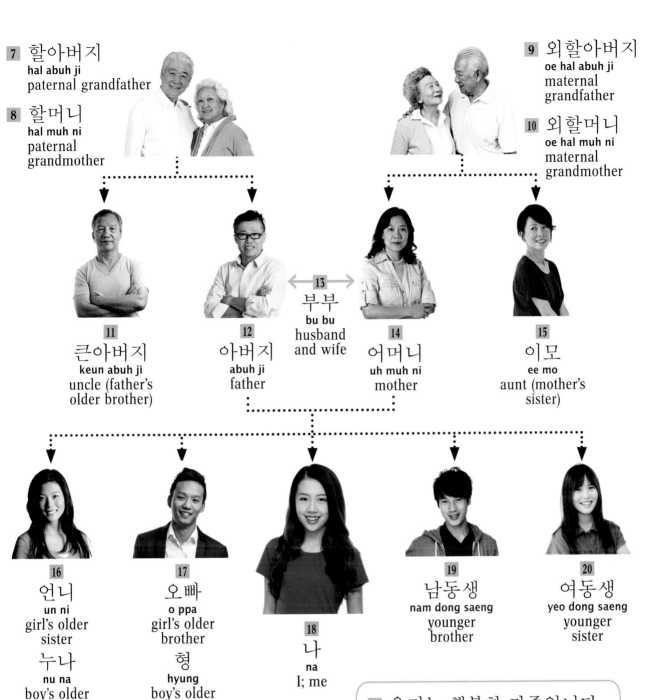

13 부부
bu bu
husband and wife

11 큰아버지
keun abuh ji
uncle (father's older brother)

12 아버지
abuh ji
father

14 어머니
uh muh ni
mother

15 이모
ee mo
aunt (mother's sister)

16 언니
un ni
girl's older sister
누나
nu na
boy's older sister

17 오빠
o ppa
girl's older brother
형
hyung
boy's older brother

18 나
na
I; me

19 남동생
nam dong saeng
younger brother

20 여동생
yeo dong saeng
younger sister

21 조카
jo ka
nephew

22 조카딸
jokattal
niece

41 우리는 행복한 가족입니다.
Uri-neun haengbokhan gajok ipnida.
We are a happy family!

11

나의 집

Naui jip

3 My House

1 거실
geo sil
living room

2 발코니
bal ko ni
balcony

3 난간
nan gan
railing

4 천장
cheon jeong
ceiling

5 열쇠
yeol swei
keys

6 그림
geu rim
painting

9 텔레비젼
tael lae bi jyeon
television

7 의자
ui ja
chair

10 탁자
tak ja
coffee table

8 벽
byeok
wall

11 카펫
ka paet
carpet

15 에어컨
ae eo keon
air conditioner

16 천정등
cheon jeong deung
ceiling light

12 식탁
sik tak
table

13 소파
so pa
sofa

14 바닥
ba dak
floor

17 커튼
keo teun
curtain

18 창문
chang mun
window

19 베개
bae gae
pillow

Additional Vocabulary

49 전등 스위치
jeondeung
seuweichi
light switch

50 전기 소켓
jeongi sokaet
electric socket;
power point

51 집
jip
house

52 아파트
a pa teu
apartment

53 지붕
ji bung
roof

54 다락방
da rak bang
attic; loft

55 지하실
ji ha sil
basement;
cellar

56 차고
cha go
garage

20 침대
chim dae
bed

21 침실
chim sil
bedroom

22 방
bang
room

57 참 아름다운 집이네요. 여기서 살았으면 좋겠네요.
Cham areumdaun jipinaeyo. yeogiseo salatsseumyeon jogaetnaeyo.
What a beautiful house. I would love to live here.

23 부엌
bu eok
kitchen

24 전자레인지
jeonjaraeinji
microwave oven

28 후드
hu deu
range hood

25 캐비닛
kae bi nit
cabinet

29 주전자
ju jeon ja
kettle

26 냉장고
naeng jang go
refrigerator

30 토스터
to seu teo
toaster

27 오븐
o beun
oven

31 스토브
seu to beu
stove

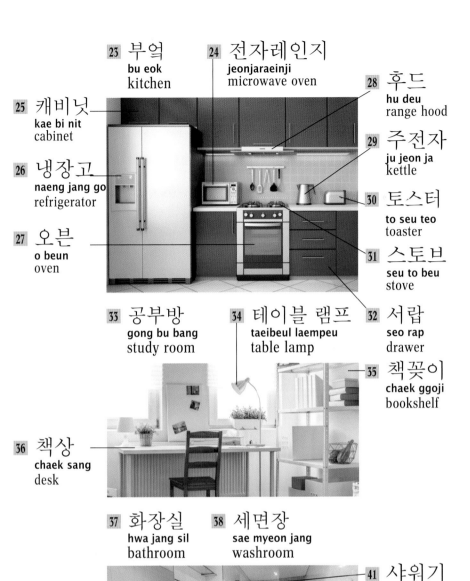

44 청소하다/
집안일
cheongsohada/jipanil
to clean/do housework

33 공부방
gong bu bang
study room

34 테이블 램프
taeibeul laempeu
table lamp

32 서랍
seo rap
drawer

35 책꽂이
chaek ggoji
bookshelf

36 책상
chaek sang
desk

45 승강기
seung gang gi
elevator

46 문
mun
door

37 화장실
hwa jang sil
bathroom

38 세면장
sae myeon jang
washroom

41 샤워기
sya wo gi
shower

47 화분 식물
hwabun sikmul
potted plant

39 수도꼭지
su do ggok ji
faucet

42 욕조
yok jo
bathtub

48 목욕하다
mokyokhada
to bathe

40 싱크대
sing keu dae
sink

43 변기
byeon gi
toilet
bowl

---

58 이집은 몇층까지 있나요?
Ijipeun myeotcheungggaji itnayo?
How many floors does this house have?

60 엄청 큰 집이네요!
Eomcheong keun jipinaeyo!
What a big house!

59 아파트를 렌트하고 싶어요.
Apateureul laenteuhago sipeoyo.
I would like to rent an apartment.

61 부엌을 보고 싶어요.
Bueokeul bogo sipeoyo.
I want to see the kitchen.

인체
In chae

4 The Human Body

6 머리카락
meo ri ka rak
hair

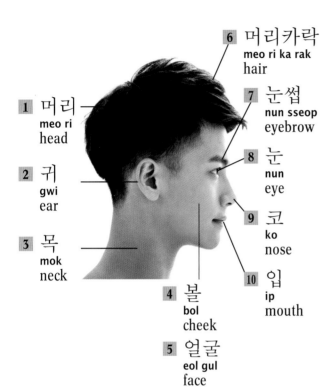

1 머리
meo ri
head

2 귀
gwi
ear

3 목
mok
neck

7 눈썹
nun sseop
eyebrow

8 눈
nun
eye

9 코
ko
nose

10 입
ip
mouth

4 볼
bol
cheek

5 얼굴
eol gul
face

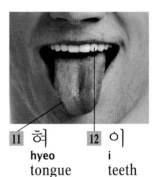

11 혀
hyeo
tongue

12 이
i
teeth

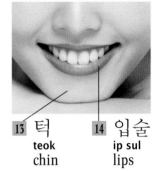

13 턱
teok
chin

14 입술
ip sul
lips

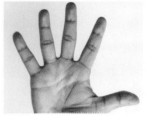

15 손가락
son ga rak
fingers

16 발가락
bal ga rak
toes

50 몸체부분을 몇개나 말할수있나요?
Momchaebubuneul myeotgaena malhalsuitnayo?
How many parts of your body can you name?

51 몸을 어떻게 관리하나요?
Momeul eoddeogae gwanrihanayo?
How do you take care of your body?

52 담배는 건강에 해롭습니다.
Dambaeneun geongangae haeropseupnida.
Smoking is bad for your health.

53 과식과 과음하지 않게 주의하세요.
Gwasikgwa gwaeumhaji ankae juuihasaeyo.
Be careful not to eat and drink too much.

54 단것과 간식을 너무하지 마세요.
Dangeotgwa gansikeul neomuhaji masaeyo.
Don't eat too many sweets and snacks.

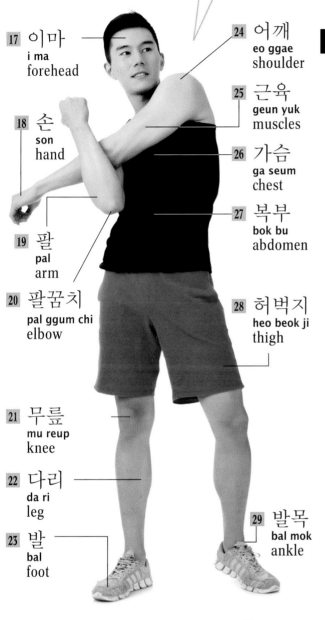

55 건강하려면 매일 운동해야해요.
Geongangharyeomyeon maeil undonghaeyahaeyo.
To stay healthy, you should exercise every day.

17 이마
i ma
forehead

24 어깨
eo ggae
shoulder

25 근육
geun yuk
muscles

18 손
son
hand

26 가슴
ga seum
chest

27 복부
bok bu
abdomen

19 팔
pal
arm

20 팔꿈치
pal ggum chi
elbow

28 허벅지
heo beok ji
thigh

21 무릎
mu reup
knee

22 다리
da ri
leg

23 발
bal
foot

29 발목
bal mok
ankle

Additional Vocabulary

36 배꼽
bae ggop
navel

37 소화
so hwa
digestion

38 눈물
nun mul
tear

39 재채기
jae chae gi
sneeze

40 호흡
ho heup
breath

41 피부
pi bu
skin

42 피
pi
blood

43 손톱
son top
fingernails

44 뼈
ppyeo
bone

45 발톱
bal top
toenails

46 수염
su yeom
beard

47 건강
geon gang
health

48 병
byeong
sickness

49 위
wi
stomach

30 뇌
nui
brain

31 폐
pae
lungs

32 심장
sim jang
heart

33 신장
sin jang
kidneys

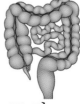

34 장
jang
intestines

35 간
gan
liver

카운팅과 숫자

Kauntinggwa sutja

Counting and Numbers

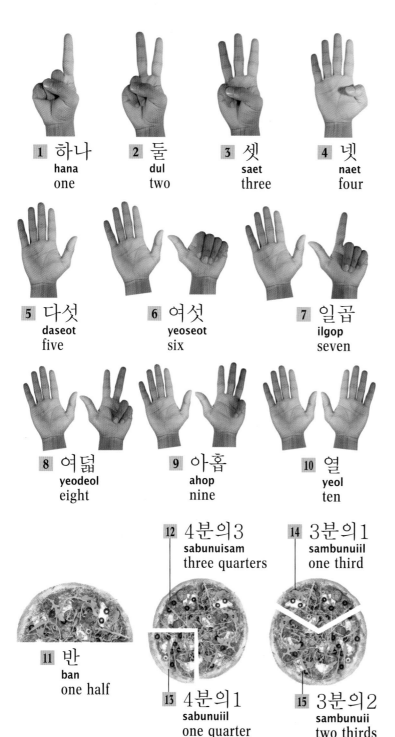

1 하나
hana
one

2 둘
dul
two

3 셋
saet
three

4 넷
naet
four

5 다섯
daseot
five

6 여섯
yeoseot
six

7 일곱
ilgop
seven

8 여덟
yeodeol
eight

9 아홉
ahop
nine

10 열
yeol
ten

12 4분의3
sabunuisam
three quarters

14 3분의1
sambunuiil
one third

11 반
ban
one half

13 4분의1
sabunuiil
one quarter

15 3분의2
sambunuii
two thirds

Cardinal Numbers 기수 **gisu**

0 제로 **jaero** zero
11 십일 **sipil** eleven
12 십이 **sipi** twelve
13 십삼 **sipsam** thirteen
14 십사 **sipsa** fourteen
15 십오 **sipo** fifteen
16 십육 **sipyuk** sixteen
17 십칠 **sipchil** seventeen
18 십팔 **sippal** eighteen
19 십구 **sipgu** nineteen
20 이십 **isip** twenty
21 이십일 **isipil** twenty-one
22 이십이 **isipi** twenty-two
23 이십삼 **isipsam** twenty-three
24 이십사 **isipsa** twenty-four
25 이십오 **isipo** twenty-five
26 이십육 **isipyuk** twenty-six
27 이십칠 **isipchil** twenty-seven
28 이십팔 **isippal** twenty-eight
29 이십구 **isipgu** twenty-nine
30 삼십 **samsip** thirty
40 사십 **sasip** forty
50 오십 **osip** fifty
60 육십 **yuksip** sixty
70 칠십 **chilsip** seventy
80 팔십 **palsip** eighty
90 구십 **gusip** ninety
100 백 **baek** one hundred
1,000 천 **cheon** one thousand
10,000 만 **man** ten thousand
100,000 십만 **sipman**
  one hundred thousand
1,000,000 백만 **baekman**
  one million
100,000,000 10억 **ileok**
  one hundred million
1,000,000,000 10억 **sipeok**
  one billion
10,000,000,000 100억 **baekeok**
  ten billion

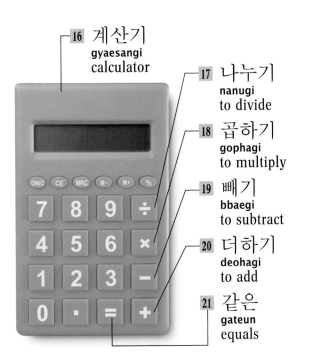

16 계산기
gyaesangi
calculator

17 나누기
nanugi
to divide

18 곱하기
gophagi
to multiply

19 빼기
bbaegi
to subtract

20 더하기
deohagi
to add

21 같은
gateun
equals

Ordinal Numbers 서수 seosu
1st 첫번째 cheotbeonjjae first
2nd 두번째 dubeonjjae second
3rd 세번째 saebeonjjae third
4th 네번째 naebeonjjae fourth
5th 다섯번째 daseotbeonjjae fifth
6th 여섯번째 yeoseotbeonjjae sixth
7th 일곱번째 ilgopbeonjjae seventh
8th 여덟번째 yeodeolbeonjjae eighth
9th 아홉번째 ahopbeonjjae ninth
10th 열번째 yeolbeonjjae tenth
11th 열한번째 yeolhanbeonjjae eleventh
12th 열두번째 yeoldubeonjjae twelfth
13th 열세번째 yeolsaebeonjjae thirteenth
20th 스무번째 seumubeonjjae twentieth
30th 서른번째 seoreunbeonjjae thirtieth
40th 마흔번째 maheunbeonjjae fortieth
50th 쉰번째 shinbeonjjae fiftieth
60th 예순번째 yaesunbeonjjae sixtieth
70th 일흔번째 ilheunbeonjjae seventieth
80th 여든번째 yeodeunbeonjjae eightieth
90th 아흔번째 aheunbeonjjae ninetieth
100th 백번째 baekbeonjjae one-hundredth
1000th 천번째 cheonbeonjjae one-thousandth

Additional Vocabulary

22 둘/양쪽
dul/yangjjok
two; both

23 퍼센트
peosaenteu
percent (%)

24 분수
bunsu
fraction

25 짝수
jjaksu
even numbers

26 홀수
holsu
odd numbers

27 세다
saeda
to count

28 숫자
sutja
numbers

29 자릿수
jaritsu
digits

30 2 더하기 4는 6이다.
I deohagi saneun yukida.
Two plus four equals six.

31 11 빼기 5는 6이다.
Sipil bbaegi oneun yukida.
Eleven minus five equals six.

32 10 곱하기 12는 120이다.
Sip gophagi sipineun baekisipida.
Ten times twelve equals one hundred and twenty.

33 42 나누기 8은 5 1/2 이다.
Sasipi nanugi paleun oae ibunuiil ida.
Forty-two divided by eight equals five and a quarter.

6 일상생활
Il sang saeng hwal
Daily Activities

5 서다
seo da
to stand

6 앉다
an daò
to sit

1 울다
ul da
to cry

2 웃다
ut da
to laugh

3 듣다
deut da
to listen

4 보다
bo da
to look; see

Additional Vocabulary

18 소리
so ri
sound

19 묻다
mut da
to ask

20 놀다
nol da
to play

21 호흡하다
ho heup ha da
to breathe

22 대답하다
dae dap ha da
answer

23 보다
bo da
to catch sight of

24 출근하다/
퇴근하다
chulgeunhada/
tweigeunhada
go to work /
get off work

25 등교하다
deung gyo ha da
go to school

26 하교
ha gyo
school is over

27 요리하다;
음식을 만들다
yorihada; eumsikeul
mandeulda
to cook; to prepare
a meal

28 샤워하다
shya wo ha da
to have a shower

29 머리 감다
meo ri gam da
to wash my hair

30 쉬다
shwi da
to relax

31 저녁 식탁
jeonyeok siktak
dining table

32 점심 먹다
jeom sim meok da
to have lunch

33 저녁 먹다
jeo nyeok meok da
to have dinner

34 여가
yeo ga
leisure

35 공부 시간
gongbu sigan
study time

36 책 읽기
chaek ilgi
reading a book

37 평일
pyeong il
weekday

38 주말
ju mal
weekend

39 매일 8시간 잠을 자야해요.
Maeil yeodeolsigan jameul jayahaeyo.
I need eight hours of sleep every day.

7 자다
ja da
to sleep

8 티비보기
ti bi bo gi
to watch TV

9 쓰다
sseu da
to write

10 일어나다
il eo na da
to wake up

11 이 닦다
i dak da
to brush teeth

12 말하다
mal ha da
to talk

13 연설하다
yeon seol ha da
to speak

15 이사하다
i sa ha da
to move

16 돕다
dop da
to help

14 모두 함께 식사합니다.
Modu hamggae siksahapnida.
Everybody eats together.

40 평일저녁에 뭐해요?
Pyeongil jeonyeokae mwohaeyo?
What do you do on weekday evenings?

41 주말에 뭐해요?
Jumalae mwohaeyo?
What do you do on weekends?

42 매일아침 무엇을 먼저해요?
Maeilachim mueotseul meonjeohaeyo?
What is the first thing you do every morning?

43 저는 샤워하고 이를 닦아요.
Jeoneun shyawohago ireul dakayo.
I take a shower and brush my teeth.

17 개 산책하기
gae sanchakhagi
to walk the dog

색상, 모양, 크기
Saeksang, moyang, keugi
Colors, Shapes and Sizes

7

1 색
saek
colors

2 빨간색
bbal gan saek
red

3 흰색
hin saek
white

4 검정색
geom jeong saek
black

5 노란색
no ran saek
yellow

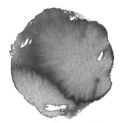

6 파란색
pa ran saek
blue

7 녹색
nok saek
green

8 보라색
bo ra saek
purple

9 갈색
gal saek
brown

10 회색
hwei saek
gray

11 오렌지색
o raen ji saek
orange

12 분홍색
bun hong saek
pink

13 금색
geum saek
gold

14 은색
eun saek
silver

15 어두운 색
eoduun saek
dark color

16 밝은 색
balgeun saek
light color

45 가장 좋아하는 색이 뭐에요?
Gajang joahaneun saeki mwoaeyo?
What is your favorite color?

46 가장좋아하는 색은 빨강이에요.
Gajangjoahaneun saekeun bbalgangiaeyo.
My favorite color is red.

17 무지개
mu ji gae
a rainbow

18 직사각형
jik sa gak hyeong
a rectangle

19 원
won
a circle

20 팔각형
pal gak hyeong
an octagon

21 오각형
o gak hyeong
a pentagon

22 정사각형
jeong sa gak hyeong
a square

23 하트
ha teu
a heart

24 타원형
ta won hyeong
an oval

25 별
byeol
a star

26 삼각형
sam gak hyeong
a triangle

27 육각형
yuk gak hyeong
a hexagon

28 마름모
ma reum mo
a diamond

29 옷 치수
ot chisu
clothing size

M SIZE

30 미디엄
mi di eom
M size

S SIZE
31 스몰
seu mol
S size

XS SIZE
32 엑스트라 스몰
aekseuteura seumol
XS size

L SIZE
33 라지
la ji
L size

XL SIZE
34 엑스트라
aekseuteura
라지
laji
XL size

35 라지
la ji
large

36 미디엄
mi di eom
medium

37 스몰
seu mol
small

43 더 큰 사이즈 있어요?
Deo keun saijeu itsseoyo?
Do you have a larger size?

Additional Vocabulary

38 색상
saek sang
color

39 모양
mo yang
shape

40 크기
keu gi
size

41 더 큰
deo keun
larger

42 더 작은
deo jakeun
smaller

44 이걸로 다른색 있어요?
Igeollo dareunsaek itsseoyo?
Do you have this in other colors?

반대들
Ban dae deul
Opposites

8

1 위 ↔ 아래
wi   a rae
up   down

2 받다 ↔ 주다
bat da   ju da
receive   give

3 많은 ↔ 적은
man eun   jeok eun
more   less

4 오래된 ↔ 새것
o rae dwen   sae geot
old   new

5 긴 ↔ 짧은
gin   jjalbeun
tall   short

6 출구 ↔ 들어가다
chul gu   deul-eogada
exit   enter

7 좋은 ↔ 나쁜
jo eun   na ppeun
good   bad

9 아름다운
a reum da un
beautiful
↕
못생긴
mot saeng gin
ugly

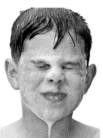

8 젖은 ↔ 마른
jeojeun   ma reun
wet   dry

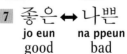

10 긴 ↔ 짧은
gin   jjalbeun
long   short

Additional Vocabulary

15 입다↔벗다
ib da   beot da
put   take
on   off

11 늙은↔젊은
neulgeun jeolmeun
old   young

12 큰↔작은
keun   jak eun
big   small

16 어려운↔쉬운
eoryeoun   swiun
difficult easy

17 있다↔없다
it da   eop da
have   do not
         have

18 오다↔가다
o da   ga da
come   go

19 네↔아니요
nae   a ni yo
yes   no

20 배부른↔배고픈
bae bu reun   bae go peun
eat till   hungry
full

21 도착↔출발
do chak   chul bal
arrive   depart

22 안↔밖
an   bak
inside outside

23 과거↔미래
gwa geo   mi rae
past   future

24 시작↔끝
si jak   ggeut
begin   end

25 가까운↔먼
ga gga un   meon
near   far

26 틀린↔맞는
teul lin   mat neun
wrong   right

27 진짜↔가짜
jin jja   ga jja
real   fake

28 빠른↔느린
ppa reun   neu rin
fast   slow

13 열린↔닫힌
yeol lin   dachin
open   closed

14 뚱뚱한↔마른
ddungddunghan   ma reun
fat   skinny

29 무례함의 반대는 친절함입니다.
Muryehamui bandaeneun chinjeolhamipnida.
The opposite of rudeness is kindness.

30 차갑고 뜨거움은 반대어 입니다.
Chagapgo ddeugeoumeun bandaeeo ibnida.
Cold and hot is also a pair of opposites.

31 더러움의 반대는 깨끗함입니다.
Deoreoumui bandaeneun ggaeggeuthamibnida.
The opposite of dirty is clean.

현금과 돈
Hyeongeumgwa don
Cash and Money

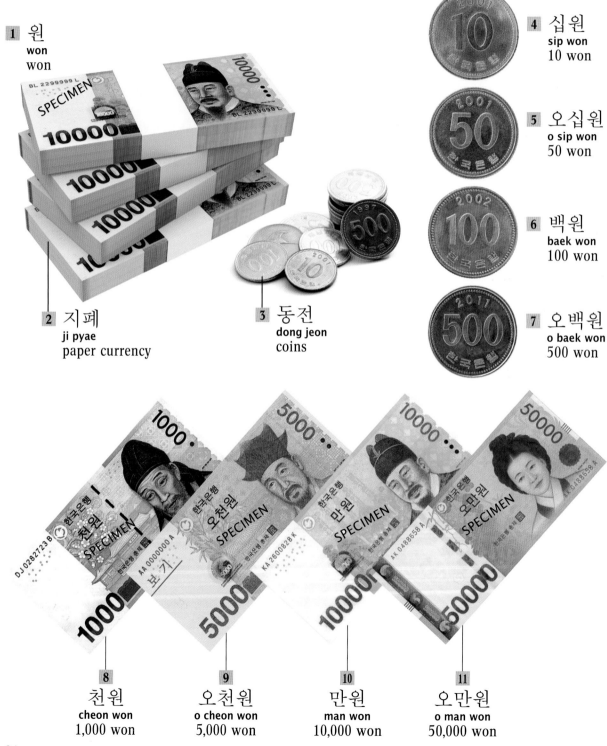

1 원
won
won

2 지폐
ji pyae
paper currency

3 동전
dong jeon
coins

4 십원
sip won
10 won

5 오십원
o sip won
50 won

6 백원
baek won
100 won

7 오백원
o baek won
500 won

8 천원
cheon won
1,000 won

9 오천원
o cheon won
5,000 won

10 만원
man won
10,000 won

11 오만원
o man won
50,000 won

12 수표
su pyo
check

13 잔돈
jan don
small change

14 신용카드
sin yong ka deu
credit card

15 저축
jeo chuk
savings

16 외화 환전
weihwa hwanjeon
currency exchange

17 인출
in chul
withdraw

18 동전; 돈
dongjeon; don
coin; money

19 가격
ga gyeok
price

20 할인
hal in
discount

21 싼
ssan
cheap

22 비싼
bi ssan
expensive

23 통장
tong jang
bankbook

24 융자
yung ja
loan

25 부채
bu chae
debt

26 예금
yea geum
deposit

27 지갑
ji gap
purse

28 영수증
yeong su jeung
receipt

29 월세
weol sae
rent

30 지갑
ji gap
wallet

31 현금
hyeon geum
cash

32 이거 얼마에요?
Igeo eolmaaeyo?
How much does this cost?

33 $24.95 요.
Isipsabul gusiposenteu yo.
Twenty-four ninety-five.

34 할인 되나요?
Halin dweinayo?
Can you give a discount?

35 네, 10% 할인이요.
Nae, sippeuro haliniyo.
OK, 10% discount.

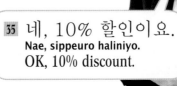

25

쇼핑하기
Syopinghagi
Going Shopping

10

4 쇼핑백
syopingbaek
shopping bag

1 사다
sada
to buy

54 얼마에요?
Eolmaaeyo?
How much is it?

2 팔다
palda
to sell

3 쇼핑하다
syopinghada
to shop

5 시계
si gyae
watch

6 옷
ot
clothes

11 안경
angyeong
glasses; spectacles

14 셔츠
syeo cheu
shirt

7 블라우스
beullauseu
blouse

12 양말
yangmal
socks

15 넥타이
naektai
necktie

9 청바지
cheongbaji
jeans

8 치마
chima
skirt

10 바지
baji
trousers

13 신발
sinbal
shoes

16 모자
moja
hat

Some useful shopping expressions:

45 근처에 쇼핑센타가 어딨나요?
Geuncheoae syopingsaentaga eoditnayo?
Where is the nearest shopping center?

46 입어봐도 돼요?
Ibeobwado dweiyo?
Can I try it on?

47 탈의실이 어디에요?
Taluisili eodiaeyo?
Where is the fitting room?

48 너무 비싸요!
Neomu bissayo!
That's too expensive!

49 할인 돼나요?
Halin dweinayo?
Can you give me a discount?

50 이걸로 할게요.
Igeollo halgaeyo.
I'll take it.

51 신용카드 받아요?
Sinyongkadeu batayo?
Do you accept credit cards?

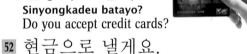

52 현금으로 낼게요.
Hyeongeumeuro naelgaeyo.
I'll pay in cash.

53 영수증 받을수 있나요?
Yeongsujeung bateulsu itnayo?
Could I have a receipt?

17 화장품
hwajangpum
cosmetics

18 장난감
jangnangam
toys

19 벨트
baelteu
belt

20 스카프
seukapeu
scarf

Additional Vocabulary

21 블랙프라이데이
beullaekpeuraidaei
Black Friday

22 가게
gagae
shop

23 백화점
baekhwajeom
department store

24 부티크
butikeu
boutique

25 점원
jeomwon
shop staff

26 계산원
gyaesanwon
cashier

27 집배원
jipbaewon
home delivery

28 가격비교
gagyeokbigyo
comparing prices

29 온라인 쇼핑
onlain syoping
online shopping

30 신용카드
sin yong ka deu
credit card

31 같은
gateun
the same as

32 모두
modu
altogether

33 분명히
bunmyeonghi
certainly

34 일반적으로
ilbanjeokeuro
generally

35 더; 훨씬 더
deo; hweolssin deo
more; even more

36 결정
gyeoljeong
decision

37 다른
dareun
other

38 가져오다
gajyeooda
to bring

39 물건들
mulgeondeul
things

40 청구서; 송장
cheongguseo;
songjang
bill; invoice

41 면세
myeonsae
tax free

42 환불
hwanbul
refund

43 이거 세금 있나요?
Igeo saegeum itnayo?
Is there any tax on this?

44 나중에 세금 환불받을수 있나요?
Najungae saegeum hwanbulbateulsu itnayo?
Can I refund the tax later?

도시의 생활

Dosiui saenghwal

Life in the City

11

1 호텔
ho tael
hotel

2 공항
gong hang
airport

3 상점
sang jeom
shop

4 거리
geo ri
street

5 슈퍼마켓
syu peo ma kaet
supermarket

6 주유소
ju yu so
gas station;
petrol station

7 은행
eun haeng
bank

8 회의장
hwei ui jang
conference center

9 기차역
gi cha yeok
train station

10 박물관
bak mul gwan
museum

11 도시
do si
city

12 고층건물
go cheung geon mul
skyscraper

13 아파트 단지
a pa teu dan ji
apartment building

14 미술관
mi sul gwan
art museum

15 경기장
gyeong gi jang
stadium

16 우체국
u chae kuk
post office

17 경찰서
gyeong chal seo
police station

18 고속도로
go sok do ro
expressway

19 헬스장
hael seu jang
gym

20 극장
geuk jang
theater

21 쇼핑
syo ping
shopping

22 도서관
do seo gwan
library

23 시청
si cheong
city hall

24 교외
gyo wei
suburb

25 아파트; 집
a pa teu; jip
apartment;
house

26 다리
da ri
bridge

27 인도
in do
sidewalk

28 이웃
i ut
neighbor

29 도로
do ro
road

30 길모퉁이
gil mo tung i
street corner

31 기념물
gi nyeom mul
monument

32 교회
gyo hwei
church

33 교통
gyo tong
traffic

34 보행자
bohaengja
pedestrian

35 횡단 보도
hoengdan bodo
pedestrian
crossing

36 사찰
sa chal
temple

37 신호등
sinhodeung
traffic lights

38 도시에 살아요? 아님 교외 살아요?
Dosiae salayo? Anim gyowei salayo?
Do you live in the city? Or in the suburbs?

39 출근을 어떻게 해요?
Chulgeuneul eoddeogae haeyo?
How do you go to work?

40 공항이 시청에서 얼마나 멀어요?
Gonghangi sicheongaeseo eolmana meoleoyo?
How far is the airport from the city hall?

41 박씨는 도시에 살기 원해요.
Pakssineun dosiae salgi wonhaeyo.
Miss Park wants to live in the city.

29

이동 수단

I dong su dan

12 | Getting Around

1 자동차
ja dong cha
car

2 택시
taek si
taxi

3 운전사
un jeon sa
driver

4 비행기
bi haeng gi
airplane

5 트럭
teu reok
truck

6 쓰레기차
sseu rae gi cha
garbage truck

7 배달용 밴
baedalyong baen
delivery van

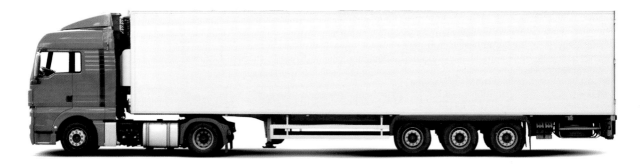

8 고속열차
go sok yeol cha
high speed train

9 오토바이
o to ba i
motorcycle

10 스포츠 카
seu po cheu ka
sports car

13 버스 정류장
beo seu jeong ryu jang
bus stop

11 지하철
ji ha cheol
subway

12 버스
beo seu
bus

14 배
bae
ship; boat

15 기차
gi cha
train

16 소방차
so bang cha
fire engine

17 전차
jeon cha
tram

18 삼륜 자전거
samryun jajeongeo
pedicab; trishaw

Additional Vocabulary

19 승객
seung gaek
passenger

20 버스타다;
beoseutada;
버스로
beoseuro
take a bus;
by bus

21 버스를 잡다
beoseureul japda
catch a bus

22 기차를 잡다
gichareul japda
catch a train

23 기차를 타다
gichareul tada
ride a train

24 차를 운전하다
chareul unjeonhada
drive a car

25 자전거를 타다
jajeongeoreul tada
ride a bike

26 줄이다
jul i da
slow down

27 빨리가다
bbal li ga da
go faster

28 좌회전/우회전
jwa hwei jeon/
u hwei jeon
turn left/turn right

29 똑바로 가다
ddok ba ro ga da
go straight

30 열차 시간표
yeolcha siganpyo
train schedule

31 나침반
na chim ban
compass

32 버스 노선
beoseu noseon
bus route

33 바퀴
ba kwi
wheel

34 택시를 부르다
taeksireul bureuda
to call a taxi

35 갈아타다
gal a ta da
transfer

36 시청으로 가는 가장좋은 방법이 뭐에요?
Sicheongeuro ganeun gajangjoeun bangbeopi mwoeyo?
What is the best way to get to city hall?

37 버스로 택시로 또는 지하철을 타세요.
Beoseuro taeksiro ddoneun jihacheoleul tasaeyo.
By bus, by taxi or take the subway.

38 기차역에 어떻게 가요?
Gichayeokae eoddeogae gayo?
How do I get to the train station?

13 방향 묻고 말하기
Banghyang mutgo malhagi
Asking and Giving Directions

1 어디?
eodi?
where?

6 북
buk
north

7 북서
bukseo
northwest

8 북동
bukdong
northeast

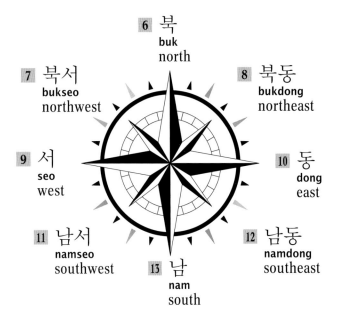

9 서
seo
west

10 동
dong
east

11 남서
namseo
southwest

13 남
nam
south

12 남동
namdong
southeast

14 앞
ap
in front

2 여기
yeogi
here

15 뒤
dwi
behind

3 거기
geogi
there

Some common phrases for asking and giving directions:

16 방향 묻기
banghyang mutgi
asking directions

21 방향 알려주기
banghyang
alryeojugi
giving directions

17 길을 잃었어요.
도와줄수 있나요?
Gileul ileotsseoyo. Dowajulsu itnayo?
I'm lost. Can you help me?

18 이쪽이 ~ 인가요?
Iljjoki ~ ingayo?
Is this the way to … ?

19 얼마나 먼가요?
Eolmana meongayo?
How far is it?

20 지도에서 보여줄수 있나요?
Jidoaeseo boyeojulsu itnayo?
Can you show me on the map?

22 죄송합니다, 몰라요.
Jweisonghapnida. Mollayo.
I'm sorry, I don't know.

23 이쪽입니다.   **24** 저쪽입니다.
Ijjokipnida.   Jeojjokipnida.
It's this way.   It's that way.

25 왼쪽/오른쪽 입니다.
Wenjjok/oreunjjok ipnida.
It's on the left/right.

26 ~ 옆이에요.
~yeopiaeyo.
It's next to …

4 위
wi
above

5 아래
arae
below

32

28 중간
junggan
middle; center

27 오른쪽
oreunjjok
right side

29 왼쪽
wenjjok
left side

30 좌회전
jwa hwei jeon
turn left

31 직진
jikjin
go straight

32 우회전
u hwei jeon
turn right

33 밖
bak
outside

34 안
an
inside

35 길잃다
gililta
to be lost

36 방향
banghyang
direction

37 거리
geori
distance

38 킬로미터
killomiteo
kilometer

39 마일
mail
mile

40 미터
miteo
meter

41 피트
piteu
foot

42 근처
geuncheo
near

43 먼
meon
far

44 반대
bandae
opposite

45 동
dong
the East

46 남
nam
the South

47 서
seo
the West

48 북
buk
the North

49 옆
yeop
side

50 근처
geuncheo
nearby

51 장소
jangso
place

52 한쪽
hanjjok
one side

53 말하다
malhada
to tell

54 지나가다
jinagada
to go through

55 떠나다
ddeonada
to leave

56 얼마나 더?
Eolmana deo?
How much longer?

57 즉시
jeuksi
immediately

58 허락하다
heorakhada
to allow

59 이미
imi
already

33

날씨 말하기
Nalssi malhagi
14 Talking About the Weather

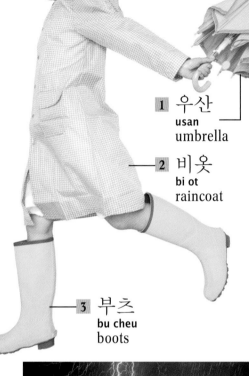

1 우산
usan
umbrella

2 비옷
bi ot
raincoat

3 부츠
bu cheu
boots

4 맑은(하늘)
malgeun (haneul)
clear (sky)

5 맑은 날
malgeun nal
clear day

6 흐린
heu rin
cloudy

7 바람
ba ram
wind

8 바람 부는
baram buneun
windy

9 비
bi
rain

10 비가 오는
biga oneun
rainy

11 번개
beon gae
lightning

12 천둥
cheon dung
thunder

13 폭풍우
pok pun goo
thunderstorm

14 눈
nun
snow

15 눈내리다
nunnaerida
to snow

16 태풍
tae pung
typhoon

38 오늘은 아름다운날 입니다. 내일은 비가 올거에요.
Oneuleun areumdaunnal ipnida. Naeileun biga olgeoaeyo.
It's a beautiful day today. Tomorrow will be rainy.

39 오늘은 아주 덥내요. 내일은 시원할 거에요.
Oneulun aju deopnaeyo. Naeileun siwonhal geoaeyo.
It is too hot today. Tomorrow will be cooler.

17 코트/자켓
koteu/jakaet
coat or jacket

18 스웨터
seuweiteo
sweater

Additional Vocabulary

31 날씨
nal ssi
weather

32 일기 예보
ilgi yaebo
weather forecast

33 좋은 날씨
jo eun nalssi
good weather

34 나쁜 날씨
nabbeun nalssi
bad weather

35 밝은 날씨
balgeun nalssi
sunny weather

36 공기오염
gonggioyeom
air pollution

37 허리케인
heorikaein
hurricane

19 더운
deo un
hot

20 더운 날씨
deo un nalssi
hot weather

21 추운
chuun
cold

22 추운 날씨
chuun nalssi
cold weather

23 구름
gu reum
cloud

24 안개
an gae
fog

25 태양
tae yang
sun

26 달
dal
moon

29 모자
moja
hat

27 호우
ho u
rainstorm

28 우박
u bak
hail

30 장갑
jang gap
gloves

35

시간 알림
Si gan al lim
Telling Time

1 시간
si gan
hour

2 분
bun
minute

3 초
cho
second

6 시계
si gyae
clock

4 정각 6시
jeong gak yeoseot si
6 o'clock

5 6시 5분
yeoseotsi o bun
five minutes
past six

8 6시 15분
yeoseotsi sipobun
fifteen minutes
past six

9 6시 30분
yeoseotsi samsipbun
half past six

7 15분
sip o bun
quarter
(hour)

35 몇시에요?
Myeotsiaeyo?
What's the time?

36 8시 30분.
Yeodeolsi samsipbun.
Half past eight.

10 7시 15분전
ilgopsi simobunjeon
fifteen minutes to
seven

11 7시 5분전
ilgopsi obunjeon
five minutes to seven

37 미안 늦었 어.
Mian neuj-eoss eo.
Sorry, I'm late.

38 괜찮아.
Gwaenchanh-a.
It's OK.

17 시간
si gan
time

18 이른 아침
il reun a chim
early morning

19 아침, 오전
a chim, o jeon
in the morning;
a.m.

20 정오
jeong o
noon

21 오후
o hu
in the afternoon;
p.m.

22 자정
ja jeong
midnight

23 항상
hang sang
all the time

24 일찍
il jjik
early

25 잠시후
jam si hu
a little later

26 어제
eo jae
yesterday

27 주말
ju mal
weekend

28 전에
jeon ae
before

29 사이에
saie
between; among

30 잠시
jam si
a brief moment

31 조금 전
jo geum jeon
a moment ago

32 과거
gwa geo
past

33 자주
ja ju
frequently

34 금방
geum hang
in a moment

12 자명종
ja myeong jong
alarm clock

13 스톱워치
seu top weo chi
stopwatch

14 스마트워치
seu ma teu weo chi
smartwatch

15 시계
si gyae
wrist watch

16 밤
bam
night

39 오후 3시에 봐요!
O hu saesiae bwayo!
See you at 3 p.m.!

16 년도와 날짜
Nyeondowa naljja
Years and Dates

4 년
nyeon
year

1 달력
dal ryeok
calendar

2 월
wal
month

3 일
il
day

JANUARY						2018
SUNDAY	MONDAY	TUESDAY	WEDNESDAY	THURSDAY	FRIDAY	SATURDAY
	New Year's Day 1	2	3	4	5	6
7	8	9	10	11	12	13
14	15	16	17	18	19	20
21	22	23	24	25	26	27
28	29	30	31			

9 일요일 il yo il Sunday
10 월요일 wal yo il Monday
11 화요일 hwa yo il Tuesday
12 수요일 su yo il Wednesday
13 목요일 mok yo il Thursday
14 금요일 geum yo il Friday
15 토요일 to yo il Saturday

5 일요일
il yo il
Sunday

6 어제
eo jae
yesterday

7 오늘
o neul
today

8 내일
nae il
tomorrow

47 일기 쓰기를 좋아해요.
Ilgi sseugireul joahaeyo.
I like to keep a diary.

48 오늘은 일월 이십육일 금요일이에요.
Oneuleun ilwal isipyukil geumyoiliaeyo.
Today is Friday, January 26.

49 어제는 일월 이십오일 목요일이었어요.
Eojaeneun ilwal isipoil mokyoilieotsseoyo.
Yesterday was Thursday, January 25.

50 내일은 일월 이십칠일 토요일이에요.
Naeileun ilwal isipchilil toyoiliaeyo.
Tomorrow will be Saturday, January 27.

How to express years, months and dates in Korean:

2018 is 이천십팔년 icheonsippalnyeon

2000 is 이천년 icheonnyeon

1994 is 천구백구십사년 cheongubaekgusipsanyeon

2013 is 이천십삼년 icheonsipsamnyeon

16 January 일월 il wal
17 February 이월 i wal
18 March 삼월 sam wal
19 April 사월 sa wal

20 May 오월 o wal
21 June 유월 yu wal
22 July 칠월 chil wal
23 August 팔월 pal wal

24 September 구월 gu wal
25 October 시월 si wal
26 November 십일월 sip il wal
27 December 십이월 sip i wal

February 5 이월 오일 iwal oil

March 31 삼월 삼십일일 samwal samsipilil

April 1 사월 일일 sawal ilil

July 4 칠월 사일 chilwal sail

December 25 십이월 이십오일 sipiwal isipoil

45 생일이 언제에요?
Saengili eonjaeaeyo?
When is your birthday?

46 제 생일은 일월 삼십일일이에요.
Jae saengileun ilwal samsipililiaeyo.
My birthday is on January 31.

Additional Vocabulary

28 작년
jak nyeon
last year

29 전년
jeon nyeon
the year before

30 올해
ol hae
this year

31 다음해
daeumhae
next year

32 후년
hu nyeon
the year after next

33 주
ju
week

34 연령
yeon ryeong
years (of age)

35 윤년
yun nyeon
leap year

36 날짜
nal jja
day of a month

37 10년
sip nyeon
decade
(10 years)

38 세기
sae gi
century
(100 years)

39 천년
cheon nyeon
millennium
(1000 years)

40 지난주
ji na ju
last week

41 전달
jeon dal
last month

42 다음주
da eum ju
next week

43 다음달
da eum dal
next month

44 일기
il gi
diary

사계절
Sa gyae jeol
Seasons of the Year

17

1 봄
bom
spring

2 여름
yeo reum
summer

3 가을
ga eul
autumn; fall

4 겨울
gyeoul
winter

5 따뜻한
dda ddeut han
warm

6 산들 바람
sandeul baram
a gentle breeze

7 복숭아꽃
bok sung a ggot
peach blossoms

8 개화하다
gae hwa ha da
to flower

9 이슬비
i seul bi
to drizzle

10 양산
yang san
sun shade

11 물 놀이
mul noli
water play

The changing colors of the seasons.
계절의 변하는 색상 gyejeol-ui byeonhaneun saegsang

봄 개화
bom gaehwa
spring blossoms

여름의 푸름
yeoreumui pureum
summer greenery

가을 단풍
gaeul danpung
autumn foliage

겨울 눈
gyeoul nun
winter snow

12 눈사람 만들기
nunsaram mandeulgi
to make a snowman

13 수확하다
su hwak ha da
to harvest

14 부채
buchae
fan

15 눈싸움
nun ssa um
snowball fights

16 선크림
seon keu rim
sunblock lotion

17 농작물
nong jak mul
crops

Additional Vocabulary

18 계절
gyae jeol
season

19 사계절
sa gyae jeol
four seasons

20 해변에가서 놀고 싶어요.
Haebyeonaegaseo nolgo sipeoyo.
I like to go to the beach and play outdoors.

21 일년에 몇계절이 있어요?
Ilnyeonae myeotgyaejeoli itsseoyo?
How many seasons are there in a year?

22 일년에 4계절이 있어요.
Ilnyeonae sagyaejeoli itsseoyo.
There are four seasons in a year.

23 어느 계절을 가장 좋아해요?
Eoneu gyaejeoleul gajang joahaeyo?
Which season do you like best?

24 가장 좋아하는 계절은 여름이에요.
Gajang joahaneun gyaejeoleun yeoreumiaeyo.
My favorite season is summer.

18 공휴일 행사
Gonghyuil haengsa
Celebrating the Holidays

1 축제, 휴일
chukjae, hyuil
festival; holiday

2 새해
sae hae
New Year

3 불꽃놀이
bul ggot nol i
fireworks

4 새해 첫날
saehae cheotnal
New Year's Day

5 부처님 오신날
bucheonim osinnal
Buddha's Birthday

6 돌
dol
first birthday

7 어린이날
eorininal
Children's Day

8 벚꽃 축제
beotggot chukjae
Cherry Blossom
Festival

9 음력 새해 전야
eumryeok saehae jeonya
Lunar New Year's Eve

10 음력 새해
eumryeok saehae
Lunar New Year

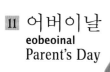

11 어버이날
eobeoinal
Parent's Day

12 발렌타인 데이
ballantain daei
Valentine's Day

Additional Vocabulary

23 생일
saeng il
birthday

24 생일 파티 참석
saengil pati chamseok
attend a birthday
party

25 여름 휴가
yeoreum hyuga
summer vacation

26 겨울 휴가
gyeoul hyuga
winter vacation

27 학교 방학
hakgyo banghak
school vacation

28 기념일
gi nyeom il
anniversary

29 백일
baek il
100th Day

30 화이트 데이
hwaiteu daei
White Day

31 블랙 데이
beullaek daei
Black Day

32 단오 축제
dano chukjae
Dano Festival

33 겨울 축제
gyeoul chukjae
winter festival

34 생일 축하합니다!
Saengil chukhahapnida!
Happy birthday!

20 선물
seon mul
gift

13 초코렛
cho ko laet
chocolates

14 장미
jang mi
roses

15 추석
chu seok
Autumn
Festival

16 송편
song pyeon
steamed
rice cake

17 할로윈
hal lo win
Halloween

35 메리 크리스마스!
Maeri keuriseumaseu!
Merry Christmas!

21 크리스마스
keu ri seu ma seu
Christmas Day

22 산타 크루즈
santa keurujeu
Santa Claus

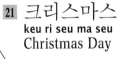

18 부활절
bu hwal jeol
Easter

19 광복절
gwang bok jeol
Independence Day

36 음력 설날맞이 함께해요.
Eumryeok seolnalmaji hamggaehaeyo.
Please join us for the Lunar New Year
celebrations.

19 배우기를 좋아해요

Baeugireul joahaeyo.

I Love to Learn

1 시험
si heom
exam

2 읽기
il gi
reading

3 배우다;
baeuda;
공부하다
gongbuhada
to learn; to study

4 수학
su hak
mathematics

5 체육
chae yuk
physical education

6 답하다
dap ha da
to answer

7 책
chaek
books

8 뉴스
nyu seu
the news

9 신문
sin mun
newspaper

10 잡지
jap ji
magazine

12 편지
pyeon ji
letter

11 사전
sa jeon
dictionary

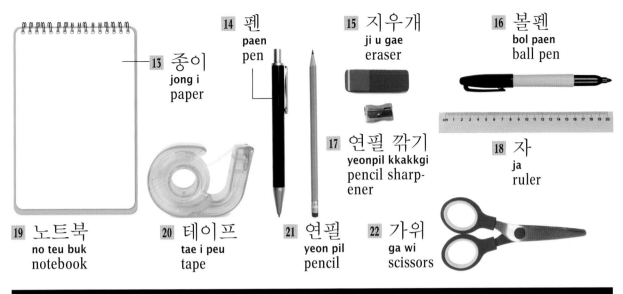

13 종이
jong i
paper

14 펜
paen
pen

15 지우개
ji u gae
eraser

16 볼펜
bol paen
ball pen

17 연필 깎기
yeonpil kkakkgi
pencil sharp-
ener

18 자
ja
ruler

19 노트북
no teu buk
notebook

20 테이프
tae i peu
tape

21 연필
yeon pil
pencil

22 가위
ga wi
scissors

Additional Vocabulary

23 학년
hak nyeon
grade; class

24 이해하다
ihaehada
to understand

25 연습하다
yeon seup ha da
to practice

26 교복
gyo bok
school
uniform

27 질문; 문제
jil mun; mun jae
a question;
problem

28 숙제
suk jae
homework

29 문학
mun hak
literature

30 역사
yeok sa
history

31 단어
dan eo
word

32 이야기
i ya gi
story

33 계산기
gyaesangi
calculator

34 사랑
sa rang
love

35 필통
pil tong
pencil case

36 과학
gwa hak
science

37 문장
mun jang
composition

38 영어
yeong eo
English

39 음악
eum ak
music

40 물리학
mul ri hak
physics

41 화학
hwa hak
chemistry

42 미술
mi sul
art

43 외국어
wui kuk eo
foreign
language

44 교실
gyo sil
classroom

45 시험
si heom
test

46 재능; 능력
jae neung;
neung ryeok
talent; ability

47 성실한;
seong sil han;
진지한
jin ji han
conscientious;
serious

48 수준
su jun
level (of
achievement)

49 향상하다
hyang sang ha da
to improve

50 책을 좋아해요!
Chaekeul joahaeyo!
I love books!

51 무슨 과목을 좋아해요?
Museun gwamokeul joahaeyo?
What is your favorite subject?

52 저는 문학과 역사를 좋아해요.
Jeoneun munhakgwa yeoksareul joahaeyo.
I like literature and history.

학교에서
Hak gyo ae seo
At School

1 화이트보드
hwa i teu bo deu
whiteboard

2 칠판
chil pan
blackboard

3 도서관
do seo gwan
library

4 교실
gyo sil
classroom

5 가르치다
ga reu chi da
to teach

6 선생님
seon saeng nim
teacher

7 복사기
bok sa gi
photocopier

9 손을 들다
soneul deulda
raise your hand

12 과학
gwa hak
science

8 복사하다
bok sa ha da
to photocopy

10 교수
gyo su
professor

11 계산기
gyaesangi
calculator

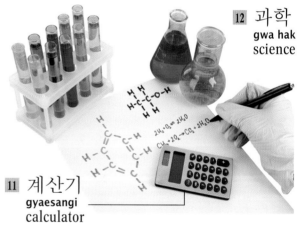

13 급우
geup u
classmates

14 강의실
gang ui sil
lecture hall

15 학생
hak saeng
student

47 과제에 도움이 필요하세요?
Gwajaee doumi pilyohasaeyo.
Do you need help with your assignment?

16 학교
hak gyo
school

17 교장
gyo jang
principal

18 강당
gang dang
auditorium

19 컴퓨터실
keom pyu teo sil
computer lab

20 실험실
sil heom sil
laboratory

21 알파벳
al pa baet
alphabet

22 성적
seong jeok
grades

23 현명한;
hyeonmyeonghan;
똑똑한
ddokddokhan
intelligent; clever

24 교과서
gyo gwa seo
textbook

25 연습장
yeon seup jang
workbook

26 초등학교 입학
cho deung hak gyo ip hak
to attend elementary school

27 초등학교
cho deung hak gyo
elementary school

28 중학교
jung hak gyo
middle school

29 고등학교
go deung hak gyo
senior high school

30 고등학교 2 학년
godeunghakgyo i haknyeon
sophomore year of high school

31 고등학교 3 학년
godeunghakgyo sam haknyeon
junior year of high school

32 고등학교 시니어
godeunghaggyo sinieo
senior year of high school

33 대학교
dae hak gyo
university; college

34 대학 1학년
daehak ilhaknyeon
freshman

35 대학 2학년
daehak ihaknyeon
sophomore year in college

36 대학 3학년
daehak samhaknyeon
junior year in college

37 대학 4학년
daehak sahaknyeon
senior year in collcge

38 야간 수업
yagan sueop
night class

39 전공하다
jeongonghada
to major

40 주제
ju jae
topic

41 졸업하다
jol eop ha da
to graduate

42 몇학년이에요?
Myeothaknyeoniaeyo?
What year are you?

43 대학 2학년이에요.
Daehak ihaknyeoniaeyo.
I'm a sophomore in college.

44 수학을 전공해요.
Suhakeul jeongonghaeyo.
I'm majoring in math.

45 전공이 뭐에요?
Jeongongi mweoaeyo?
What is your major?

46 똑똑하신 가봐요!
Ddokddokhasin gabwayo!
You must be very smart!

한글 배우기

Hangeul baeugi

21 | I Am Learning Korean

1 한글은 읽기 어려운 언어가 아닙니다.
Hangeuleun ilgi eoryeoun eoneoga anipnida.
Korean is not a difficult language to read.

2 하지만 24글을 배우는데 시간이 걸립니다.
Hajiman seumeulnaegaegeuleul baeuneundae sigani geolripnida.
But it takes time to learn the 24 letters.

The 24 letters in Korean are:

Consonants

ㄱ	ㄴ	ㄷ	ㄹ	ㅁ	ㅂ	ㅅ
\k, g\	\n\	\t, d\	\r, l\	\m\	\p, b\	\s, sh\
kiyok	niun	tikut	riul	mium	piup	siot

ㅇ	ㅈ	ㅊ	ㅋ	ㅌ	ㅍ	ㅎ
\ng\	\ch, j\	\ch\	\k\	\t\	\p, f\	\h\
iung	chiut	chiut	kiuk	tiut	piup	hiut

Vowels

ㅏ	ㅑ	ㅓ	ㅕ	ㅗ	ㅛ	ㅜ
\a\	\ya\	\eo\	\yeo\	\o\	\yo\	\u\

ㅠ	ㅡ	ㅣ
\yu\	\eu\	\i\

3 서법
seo beop
calligraphy

4 한글
hangeul
Korean character

5 자음
jaeum
consonant

6 모음
moeum
vowel

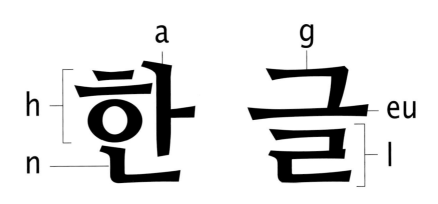

8 문자를 모두 배우는 것은 쉽습니다.
Munjareul modu baeuneun geos-eun swibseubnida.
And learning all the written characters is easy.

7 플래시 카드
peullaesi kadeu
flash cards

Additional Vocabulary

9 한국말
hankukmal
Korean language

10 억양
eok yang
accent

11 숙어
sukeo
idiom

12 문장
munjang
sentence

13 구절
gujeol
phrase

14 짧은논문
jjalbeunnonmun
short essay

15 시
si
poem

16 에세이
aesaei
essay

17 문화
munhwa
culture

18 문법
munbeop
grammar

19 번역
beonyeok
translation

20 언어학
eoneohak
linguistics

21 수업
sueop
lesson

22 과목
gwamok
course

23 연습
yeonseup
practice

24 연습장
yeonseupjang
exercise book

25 간단
gandan
simple

26 이해하다
ihaehada
to understand

27 쉬운
swiun
easy

28 어려운
eoryeoun
difficult

29 훈련하다
hunryeonhada
to drill

30 노력하다
nolyeoghada
to strive

31 준비하기
junbihagi
to prepare

수분류어

Su bun ryu eo

22 | Counting Words

1 종이두장
jong i du jang
two pieces of paper

2 책 세권
chaek saegwon
three books

3 건물 두채
geonmul duchae
two buildings

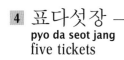

4 표다섯장
pyo da seot jang
five tickets

5 옷 여덟벌
ot yeodeolbeol
eight pieces of clothing

6 국 한그릇
guk hangeureut
one bowl of soup

7 차세대
cha sae dae
three cars

8 의자 한개
uija hangae
one chair

Some common measure words in Korean

Counting words or measure words are used to quantify things, just as in English when we say "three sheets of paper" or "two cups of coffee." However, in Korean, they put the noun first. So it looks like this: "coffee, two cups."

MEASURE WORDS	MAIN USES	EXAMPLES
벌 beol	옷 ot clothing	옷 세벌 ot saebeol *three pieces of clothing*
척 cheok	배 bae boats or ships	배 두척 bae ducheok *two boats*
채 chae	집 jip houses	집 네채 jip naechae *four houses*
다발 dabal	꽃 ggot flowers or plants	꽃 다섯 다발 ggot daseot dabal *five flowers*
그루 geuru	나무 namu trees	나무 한그루 namu hangeuru *one tree*
권 gwon	책 chaek books	책 열권 chaek yeolgwon *ten books*
마리 mari	동물 dongmul animals	개 세마리 gae saemari *three dogs*
명 myeong	사람 saram people	다섯명 daseotmyeong *five people*
켤레 kyeollae	양말 yangmal socks	양말 두켤레 yangmal dukyeollae *two pairs of socks*
점 jeom	그림 geurim paintings	그림 한점 geurim hanjeom *one painting*

11 사층 건물
sacheung geonmul
four-story building

9 사람 한그룹
saram hangeurup
one group of people

10 여섯 명
yeoseot myeong
six people

12 티 두잔
ti dujan
two cups of tea

51

23

컴퓨터와 인터넷
Keompyuteowa inteonaet
Computers and the Internet

1 컴퓨터
keom pyu teo
computers

2 스크린
seu keu rin
screen

3 테블릿
tae beul lit
tablet

7 한국에서 인터넷접속은 쉬워요.
Hankukaeseo inteonaetjeopsokeun swewoyo.
It is easy to get online in Korea.

4 피씨
pi ssi
PC

5 키보드
ki bo deu
keyboard

6 노트북
no teu buk
laptop

10 마우스
ma u seu
mouse

8 비디오 게임
bidio gaeim
video game

9 마우스 패드
mauseu paedeu
mousepad

11 스캔하다
seukaenhada
to scan

12 씨디/디비디
ssidi/dibidi
CD/DVD

13 유에스비 드라이브
yuaeseubi deuraibeu
USB flash drive

14 포트
po teu
ports

15 이메일
i mae il
email

Additional Vocabulary

16 사인하다
sa in ha da
to sign in

17 비밀번호
bi mil beon ho
password

18 웹사이트
wep sa i teu
website

19 소프트웨어
so peu teu wei eo
software

20 운영 체제
unyeong chaejae
operating system

21 바이러스
ba i reo seu
virus

22 파일
pa il
file

23 온라인
onlain
online

24 네트워킹
naeteuwoking
networking

25 호환 가능한
hohwan ganeunghan
compatible

26 와이파이
waipai
wifi

27 애플리케이션 (컴퓨터 프로그램)
aepeullikaeisyeon (keompyuteo peurogeuraem)
application (computer program)

28 인터넷
inteonaet
Internet

29 클릭하다
keullikhada
to click

30 내려받다
nae ryeo bat da
to download

31 (인터넷) 접속하다
(inteonaet) jeopsokhada
to go online

32 대화방
dae hwa bang
chat room

33 네트워크 카드
naeteuweokeu kadeu
network card

34 멀티미디어
meol ti mi di eo
multimedia

35 블로그
beul lo geu
blog

36 브라우저
beu ra u jeo
browser

37 온라인 채팅하다
onlain chaetinghada
to chat online

38 핀 코드
pin kodeu
PIN code

39 이메일 보내다
imaeil bonaeda
to send email

40 앱
aep
app

41 온라인 서치
onlain sseochi
online search

42 웹 주소/유알엘
wep juso/yualael
web address/URL

43 제 취미는 온라인 게임입니다.
Jae chimineun onlain gaeimipnida.
My hobby is online gaming.

44 온라인에서 채팅합시다.
Onlainaeseo chaetinghapsida.
Let's chat online.

45 무슨 앱을 사용해요?
Museun aepeul sayonghaeyo?
저는 앰에스앤 메신져를 이용해요.
Jeoneun aemaeseuaen maesinjyeoreul iyonghaeyo.
What app do you use? I use MSN Messenger.

46 오케이, 서류를 컴퓨터로 지금 보내는 중입니다.
Okaei, seoryureul keompyuteoro jigeum bonaeneun jung ipnida.
Okay, I'm now sending you the documents via computer.

53

스마트폰이 좋아요!
Seumateuponi joayo!
I Love My Smartphone!

24

1 스마트폰
seu ma teu pon
smartphone

2 온라인 친구들
onlain chingudeul
online friends

3 온라인 쇼핑
onlain syoping
online shopping

4 인터넷 카페
inteonaet kapae
Internet cafes

5 트위터
teu wi teo
Twitter

6 카카오토크
kakaotokeu
Kakao Talk

7 안드로이드 폰
andeuroideu pon
Android phones

8 애플 폰
aepeul pon
Apple phones

9 휴대폰
hyu dae pon
mobile phone

10 전화를 걸다
jeonhwareul geolda
to make a telephone call

11 전화를 받다
jeonhwareul batda
to answer the phone

Additional Vocabulary

24 전화번호
jeonhwa beon ho
telephone number

25 네트워크;
naeteuwokeu;
인터넷
inteonaet
network; Internet

26 인터넷 언어
inteonaet eoneo
Internet language

27 텍스팅
taek seu ting
texting

28 인터넷 은어
inteonaet euneo
Internet slang

29 전화 충전기
jeonhwa chungjeongi
phone charger

30 전화카드
jeonhwakadeu
phone cards

31 장거리 통화
janggeori tonghwa
long distance call

32 나라 번호
nara beonho
country code

33 지역 번호
jiyeok beonho
area code

34 비디오
bidio
video

35 심카드
sim ka deu
SIM card

12 강한 신호
ganghan sinho
strong signal

13 약한 신호
yakhan sinho
weak signal

14 셀피
sael pi
selfie

15 위피
wei pi
wefie

16 지마켓
ji ma kaet
Gmarket

17 네이버
nae i beo
Naver

18 페이스북
pae i seu bok
Facebook

19 구글
gu geul
Google

20 한게임
han gae im
Hangame

21 야후
ya hu
Yahoo

22 애플
ae peul
Apple

23 마이크로소프트
maikeurosopeuteu
Microsoft

Some common telephone phrases:

36 여보세요?/저는 (이름).
Yeobosaeyo?/Jeoneun (ireum).
Hello?/This is (name).

37 (이름) 통화할수있나요?
(Ireum) tonghwahalsuitnayo?
May I speak to (name)?

38 그/그녀에게 저에게 전화하라고 해주세요.
Geu/Geunyeoaegae jeoaegae jeonhwaharago haejusaeyo.
Please ask him/her to return my call.

39 지금 통화 괜찮아요?
Jigeum tonghwa gwenchanayo?
Is it convenient to talk now?

40 크게 말할수있나요?
Keugae malhalsuitnayo?
Could you speak up?

41 죄송합니다, 잘못 걸었습니다.
Jwesonghapnida. Jalmot geoleotseupnida.
Sorry, you dialed the wrong number.

42 잠시만 기다려주세요.
Jamsiman gidaryeojusaeyo.
Please wait a moment.

43 메세지를 남겨주세요.
Maesaejireul namgyeojusaeyo.
Please leave a message.

44 누구세요? Nugusaeyo?
Who's calling, please?

45 좀 천천히 말할수있나요?
Jom cheoncheonhi malhalsuitnayo?
Could you speak a little slower?

직업

Jik eop

25 At Work

1 변호사
byeon ho sa
lawyer

2 판사
pan sa
judge

9 전화 교환 원
jeonhwa gyohwan won
telephone operator

10 과학자
gwa hak ja
scientist

3 목사
mok sa
pastor

4 기술자
gi sul ja
engineer

15 사무실
sa mu sil
office

5 작가
jak ga
writer

6 간호사
gan ho sa
nurse

7 예술가
yae sul ga
artist

8 음악가
eum ak ga
musician

16 부장
bu jang
manager

17 비서
bi seo
secretary

11 요리사
yo ri sa
chef

12 종업원
jong eop won
waiter

13 공무원
gong mu won
civil servant

14 치과의사
chi gwa ui sa
dentist

18 공사장 인부
gong sa jang in bu
construction worker

19 농부
nong bu
farmer

Additional Vocabulary

20 회사
hui sa
company

21 경찰관
gyeong chal
gwan
police officer

22 수표
su pyo
to check

23 출근
chul geun
going to work

24 부사장
bu sa jang
vice president

25 작업
jak eop
work

26 직원
jik won
employee

27 기술자
gi sul ja
technician

28 사장
sa jang
CEO

29 아르바이트
a reu ba i teu
part time

30 고용
go yong
employment

31 가게 주인
ga gae ju in
shop owner

32 무슨 일을 하세요? 저는 병원에서 일해요.
Museun ileul hasaeyo? Jeoneun byeongwonaeseo ilhaeyo.
What sort of work do you do? I work in a hospital.

33 저는 의사가 되기위해 훈련하고있습니다.
Jeoneun uisaga dwaegiwihae hunryeonhago itsseumnida.
I'm training to be a doctor.

34 저는 매일 아침 8:45에 출근합니다.
Jeoneun maeil achim yeodeolsi sasimobune chulgeunhamnida.
I go to work at 8:45 a.m. every morning.

음악과 무용
Eumakgwa muyong

26 | Music and Dance

1 기타
gi ta
guitar

2 하프
hapeu
harp

3 바이올린
ba i ol lin a
violin

4 탬버린
taembeolin
tambourine

5 북
buk
drum

6 종
jong
bell

7 춤추다
chum chu da
to dance

8 가야금
gayageum
Korean zither-like
string instrument

9 피아노
piano
piano

10 트럼펫
teuleompes
trumpet

11 가라오케
ga ra o kae
karaoke

12 노래하다
noraehada
to sing

19 감상하다;
gamsanghada;
즐기다
jeulgida
to appreciate;
to enjoy

20 음악
eum ak
music

21 무용
mu yong
dance
(performance art)

22 공연
gong yeon
performance

23 프로그램
peu ro geu raem
program

24 대중 음악
dae jung eum ak
pop music

25 앨범
ael beom
album

26 음악 공연
eumak gongyeon
musical
performance

27 가수
ga su
singer

28 재즈
jae jeu
jazz

29 클래식
keul lae sik
classical

30 악기
ak gi
instrument

31 대중 문화
daejung munhwa
pop culture

32 음성
eum seong
voice

33 노래
no rae
song

13 연주회
yeon ju hwei
concert

14 청중
cheongjung
audience

15 오페라
o pae ra
opera

16 배우
bae u
actor

17 첼로
chello
cello

18 연기자
yeon gi ja
performer

34 기타를 칠수 있나요?
Gitareul chilsu itnayo?
Can you play the guitar?

35 무슨 음악을 좋아하세요?
Museun eumakeul joahasaeyo?
What kind of music do you like?

59

의사 방문
Ui sa bang mun
Seeing a Doctor

3 간호사
gan ho sa
nurse

4 의사
ui sa
doctor

5 환자
hwan ja
patient

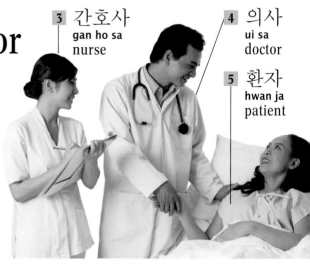

1 병원
byeong won
hospital

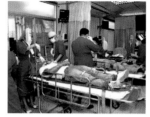

2 응급실
ueng geup shil
emergency room

6 피 뽑다
pi ppobda
to draw blood

7 피 검사
pi geomsa
blood test

8 실험실 검사
shilheomshil geomsa
laboratory test

9 혈압
hyeol ab
blood pressure

10 감기 걸리다
gamgi geollida
to catch a cold

11 기침하다
gichimhada
to cough

12 열
yeol
fever

13 병들다
byeongdeulda
to fall sick

14 약먹다
yakmeokda
to take
medicine

15 약
yak
medicine

16 알약
al yak
pills

17 주사
jusa
injection

18 상담실
sangdamshil
doctor's consultation
room

Additional Vocabulary

19 대기실
daegishil
waiting room

20 예약
yaeyak
appointment

21 구급차
gugeubcha
ambulance

22 치과
chigwa
dentistry

23 내과
naegwa
general medicine

24 외과
wuigwa
general surgery

25 이빈후과
i bin hu gwa
ear, nose and throat

26 소아과
so a gwa
pediatrics

27 산부인과
san bu in gwa
gynecology

28 안과
angwa
ophthalmology

29 피부과
pibugwa
dermatology

30 종양학
jong yang hak
oncology

31 물리치료
mul li chi ryo
physiotherapy

32 신경학
sin kyeong hak
neurology

33 방사선과
bang sa seon gwa
radiology

34 사고
sa go
accident

35 처방
cheo bang
prescription

36 소독제
so dok jae
antiseptic

37 연고
yeon go
ointment

38 상처
sang cheo
wound; cut

39 비상
bi sang
emergency

40 아파
apa
hurts

41 피곤한; 닳은
pigonhan; dalh-eun
tired; worn out

42 느낌
neukkim
to feel

43 부터
buteo
from

44 여러번
yeoleobeon
several times

45 불안한; 걱정
bul-anhan; geogjeong
anxious; worried

46 발견하는
balgyeonhaneun
to discover

47 안심할 것
ansimhal geos
to feel reassured

48 걱정할 것
geogjeonghal geos
to be concerned about

49 에 관한
e gwanhan
pertaining to

50 구급 상자
gugeub sangja
first aid kit

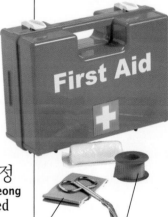

51 붕대
bungdae
bandage

52 반창고
ban chang go
adhesive tape

53 무엇이 문제입니까?
Mueosi munjeipnikka?
What is wrong?

54 열나고 목이 아픕니다.
Yeolnago moki apeubnida.
I have a fever and sore throat.

55 몸이 안좋아요.
Momi anjoayo.
I am not feeling well.

56 의사를 봐야겠어요.
Uisareul bwayagetsseoyo.
I would like to see a doctor.

57 예약을 하였습니까?
Yeyakeul hayeosseumnikka?
Do you have an appointment?

61

환경 보호
Hwan gyeong bo ho

28 | Protecting Our Environment

1 정원
jeong won
garden

2 꽃
ggot
flower

6 전동차
jeon dong cha
electric car

3 공원
gong won
park

4 오염
o yeom
pollution

5 풀
pul
grass

7 바다
ba da
ocean

8 강
gang
river

9 태양 에너지
taeyang aeneoji
solar energy

10 조용한
jo yong han
quiet

32 이곳 공기는 정말 신선하다.
Igot gonggineun jeongmal sinseonhada.
The air here is really fresh!

12 풍력
pung ryeok
wind energy

11 공기
gong gi
air

13 숲
sup
forest

14 나무
na mu
tree

15 천연 가스
cheon yeon ga seu
natural gas

16 원자력
won ja ryeok
nuclear energy

17 깨끗한
ggae ggeut han
clean

18 항구
hang gu
harbor

19 재활용
jae hwal yong
recycling

20 바위
ba wi
rocks

21 흙
heuk
soil

22 모래
mo rae
sand

23 하늘
ha neul
sky

24 씨앗
ssi at
seeds

25 화분
hwa bun
flower pot

26 빗물
bit mul
rainwater

27 청정
cheong jeong
clean

28 환경
hwan gyeong
environment

29 나뭇잎
na mut ip
leaf

30 변화
byeon hwa
changes

31 지구; 땅
ji gu; ddang
earth; ground

34 유리,종이, 플라스틱을 재활용해요.
Yuri, jongi, peullaseutikeul jaehwalyonghaeyo.
I recycle glass, paper and plastic.

33 재활용하세요?
Jaehwalyong hasaeyo?
Do you recycle?

동물의 세계
Dongmului saegye
29 | The Animal Kingdom

3 기린
gilin
giraffe

1 동물원
dongmul-won
zoo

2 얼룩말
eollugmal
zebra

32 오징어가 보여요.
Ojingeoga boyeoyo.
I see a squid.

33 강아지를 보세요.
Gangajireul bosaeyo.
Look at the puppy.

34 바퀴벌레가 있어요.
Bakwibeolraega itseoyo.
There is a cockroach.

4 호랑이
ho rang i
tiger

5 사자
sa ja
lion

6 원숭이
won sung i
monkey

7 곰
gom
bear

8 사슴
sa seum
deer

9 오리
o ri
duck

10 닭
dak
chicken

11 토끼
to kki
rabbit

12 개구리
gae gu ri
frog

13 마우스
ma u seu
mouse

14 염소
yeomso
goat

15 양
yang
sheep

16 소
so
cow

17 코끼리
ko kki ri
elephant

18 말
mal
horse

19 늑대
neuk dae
wolf

20 비둘기
bi dul gi
pigeon

21 까치
kka chi
magpie

22 새
sae
bird

23 용
yong
dragon

24 뱀
baem
snake

25 개
gae
dog

26 고양이
go yang i
cat

27 모기
mo gi
mosquito

28 파리
pa ri
housefly

29 벌
beol
bee

30 나비
na bi
butterfly

31 물고기
mul go gi
fish

건강하게 지냅시다!

Geonganghagae jinaepsida!

Let's Keep Fit!

1 탁구
tak gu
table tennis

2 축구하다
chukgu hada
to play soccer

3 레슬링
lae seul ling
wrestling

4 등산
deung san
mountain climbing

5 배드민턴
bae deu min teon
badminton

6 운동
un dong
to exercise

7 야구
ya gu
baseball

8 태권도
taekwondo
taekwondo

9 달리기
dal li gi
running

10 먼거리 달리기
meongeori dal li gi
long-distance running

11 자전거
ja jeon geo
bicycle

12 자전거 타다
jajeongeo tada
to cycle

13 시합
si hab
competition

14 결승선
gyeol seung seon
finishing line

15 골프
gol peu
golf

16 아이스케이팅
a i seu kayiting
ice-skating

17 스키
seu ki
skiing

18 조정
jo jeong
rowing

19 수영
su yeong
swimming

Additional Vocabulary

25 운동복
un dong bok
sports shirt;
sweatshirt

26 운동화
un dong hwa
sports shoes;
sneakers

27 공
gong
ball

28 건강
geon gang
healthy

20 배구
bae gu
volleyball

21 산책
san chaek
walking

22 테니스
tae ni seu
tennis

23 라켓
la kaet
racket

29 운동을 좋아합니까?
Undongeul joahabnikka?
Do you like to exercise?

30 무슨 운동을 하세요?
Museun undongeul hasaeyo?
What sports do you play?

31 산책과 농구를 좋아해요.
Sanchaekgwa nonggureul joahaeyo.
I like to jog and play basketball.

24 농구하다
nong gu hada
play basketball

여행을 좋아하세요?
Yeohaengeul joahasaeyo?
Do You Like to Travel?

31

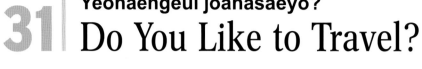

3 관광객
gwan gwang gaek
tourist

4 짐
jim
luggage

1 호텔
ho tael
hotel

2 지도
ji do
map

5 여행 안내자
yeohaeng annaejau
tour guide

6 여행지역
yeohaeng jiyeok
tourist attraction

7 여권
yeo gwon
passport

8 비행 여행
bihaeng yeohaeng
travel by airplane

9 지하철 여행
jihacheol yeohaeng
travel by subway

10 외국인
wei kuk in
foreigner

11 관광 버스
gwan gwang beo seu
tourist bus

12 호수
ho su
lake

13 카메라
ka mae ra
camera

14 사진
sa jin
photograph

Additional Vocabulary

15 여행하다
yeo haeng ha da
trip; to travel

16 수영장
su yeong jang
pool

17 휴가
hyu ga
vacation

18 신혼여행
sin hon yeo haeng
honeymoon

19 소풍
so pung
picnic

20 통화
tong hwa
currency

21 방
bang
room

22 일기
il gi
diary; journal

23 대행사
dae haeng sa
agency

24 섬
seom
island

25 시냇물
si naet mul
stream

26 시내
si nae
town

27 관광
gwan gwang
sightseeing

28 대사관
dae sa gwan
embassy

29 엽서
yeop seo
postcard

30 카페
ka pae
cafe

31 박물관
bak mul gwan
museum

32 바닷가
ba dat ga
beach

33 기념물
gi nyeom mul
monument

34 기차역
gi cha yeok
train station

35 공항
gong hang
airport

36 바닷물
ba dat mul
sea water

37 찻집
chat jip
tearoom

38 식당
sik dang
restaurant

39 찾다
chat da
to find

40 가져가다
ga jyeo ga da
to take

41 우연히 만나다
u yeon hi man na da
to come across

42 주의하다
ju ui ha da
to pay attention to

43 감지하다
gam ji ha da
to become aware of

44 짐 싸다
jim ssa da
to pack

45 도착
do chak
arrival

46 어디로 여행가고 싶으세요?
Eodiro yeohaenggago sipeusaeyo?
Where do you like to go on vacation?

47 서울에 가고싶어요.
Seoulae gago sipeoyo.
I like to go to Seoul.

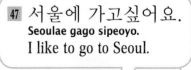

48 부산으로 돌아가는 이등석표 주세요.
Busaneuro dolaganeun ideungseokpyo jusaeyo.
I'd like a second class return train ticket to Busan.

49 그는 대전시내를 비행했습니다.
Geuneun daejeonsinaereul bihaenghaetseumnida.
He flew the area around Daejon City.

50 같은 비행기를 타고 싶습니다.
Gateun bihaenggireul tago sipseupnida.
I like to fly on the same airline.

세계 각국

Saegyae gakkuk

32 | Countries of the World

1 동남아시아
Dongnam a si a
Countries in Southeast Asia

2 태국
Taeguk
Thailand

3 미얀마
Mi yan ma
Myanmar

4 베트남
Bae teu nam
Vietnam

5 필리핀
Pil li pin
Philippines

6 라오스
La o seu
Laos

7 캄보디아
Kam bo di a
Cambodia

8 말레이시아
Mal lae i si a
Malaysia

9 브루나이
Beu ru na i
Brunei

10 싱가포르
Sing ga po reu
Singapore

11 인도네시아
In do nae si a
Indonesia

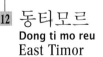

12 동티모르
Dong ti mo reu
East Timor

---

30 한국에 가봤어요? 한국에 가고 싶어요.
Hankukae gabwatssseoyo? Hankukae gago sipeoyo.
Have you been to Korea? I'd love to go to Korea.

31 어느나라에서 왔어요? 저는 미국사람입니다.
Eoneunaraaeseo watsseoyo? Jeoneun mikuksaramipnida.
What country are you from? I am American.

13 세계 7 대륙
saegyae chi daeryuk
Seven continents of the world

14 북아메리카
Bukamaerika
North America

15 남아메리카
Namamaerika
South America

16 유럽
Yu reop
Europe

17 아프리카
A peu ri ka
Africa

18 아시아
A si a
Asia

19 오스트레일리아
O seu teu rae il li a
Australia

20 남극
Nam geuk
Antartica

21 일본
Il bon
Japan

22 한국
Han kuk
Korea

23 중국
Jung kuk
China

24 미국
Mi kuk
America

25 인도
In do
India

26 호주
Ho ju
Australia

27 이탈리
Il tal li
Italy

캐나다 **Kae na da** Canada
덴마크 **Daen ma keu** Denmark
프랑스 **Peu rang seu** France
독일 **Dok il** Germany
영국 **Yeong kuk** Great Britain
아일랜드 **A il laen deu** Ireland
룩셈부르크 **Luk saem bu reu keu**
 Luxembourg
네덜란드 **Nae deol lan deu**
 Netherlands

뉴질랜드 **Nyu jil laen deu**
 New Zealand
노르웨이 **No reu wei i** Norway
폴란드 **Pollandeu** Poland
러시아 제국 **Eosia jegug** Russia
스웨덴 **Seuweden** Sweden

Additional Vocabulary

28 지구
ji gu
globe

29 세계
sae gyae
world

71

외국어
Wei kuk eo

33 Foreign Languages

Hello!

1 영어
Yeong eo
English

Bonjour!

2 프랑스어
Peu rang seu eo
French

привет

3 러시아어
Leo si a eo
Russian

4 독일어
Dok il eo
German

Guten Tag!

Ciao!

5 이탈이어
I tal i eo
Italian

¡Hola!

6 서반어
Seo ban eo
Spanish

Merhaba!

こんにちは

مرحبا

7 터키어
Teo ki eo
Turkish

8 일본어
Il bon eo
Japanese

9 아랍어
A rab eo
Arabic

10 그리스어
Geu ri seu eo
Greek

11 히브리어
Hi beu ri eo
Hebrew

12 베트남어
Bae teu nam eo
Vietnamese

13 힌두어
Hin du eo
Hindi

14 인도네시아어
In do ne si a eo
Indonesian

15 타이어
Ta i eo
Thai

17 타갈로그어
Ta gal ro geu eo
Tagalog

18 포르투갈어
Po reu tu gal eo
Portuguese

19 중국어
Jung kuk eo
Mandarin
Chinese

16 한국말
Han kuk mal
Korean

20 모국어가 뭐에요?
Mokukeoga mueoeyo?
What is your mother tongue?

21 몇개 언어를 말해요?
Myeotgae eoneoreul malhaeyo?
How many languages do you speak?

34 한국음식을 좋아하세요?
Hankukeumsikeul joahasaeyo?
Do You Like Korean Food?

1 한국 식당
hankuk sikdang
Korean restaurant

2 종업원
jong eop won
waiter; waitress

3 요리사
yo ri sa
cook; chef

4 메뉴
mae nyu
menu

5 김치
kim chi
Kimchi

6 죽
juk
rice porridge

7 설렁탕
seol reol tang
beef soup with rice

8 젓가락
jeot ga rak
chopsticks

13 포크
po keu
fork

14 칼
kal
knife

9 그릇
geu reut
bowl

10 밥; 쌀
bap; ssal
rice

11 흰밥
huin bap
white rice

12 접시
jeop si
plate

15 숟가락
sut ga rak
spoon

16 비빔밥
bi bim bap
dish of steamed rice,
vegetables, egg and meat

17 송편
song pyeon
rice cake steamed
over pine needles

18 만두
man du
dumplings

19 삼계탕
samgyetang
ginseng chicken
soup

20 자장면
ja jang myeon
black Chinese noodles

21 칼국수
kal kuk su
knife-cut noodles

22 떡볶이
tteokbokki
stir-fried rice cake

23 반찬
banchan
side dishes

24 불고기
bulgogi
marinated grilled
meat

25 잡채
japchae
stir-fried glass
noodles

Additional Vocabulary

26 국
kuk
soup

27 김밥
gimbap
seaweed rice roll

28 파전
pajeon
green onion
pancake

29 고구마
go gu ma
sweet potato

30 인삼
in sam
ginseng

31 주문하다
ju mun ha da
to order

32 모두 한국 음식을 좋아합니다.
Modu hankuk eumsikeul joahapnida.
Everyone likes to eat Korean food.

33 오늘 저녁 초대할게요.
Oneul jeonyeok chodaehalgaeyo.
Today, I will invite you to dinner.

34 좋아요. 한국음식을 먹고 싶어요.
Joayo. Hankukeumsikeul meokgo sipeoyo.
That's great! I want to eat Korean food.

대중 서양 음식

Daejung seoyang eumsik

Popular Western Foods

35

1 핫도그
hat do geu
hot dog

2 샌드위치
saen deu wi chi
sandwich

3 피자
pi ja
pizza

4 파스타;
pasueta;
스파게티
seupagaeti
pasta; spaghetti

5 도너츠
do neo cheu
donuts

6 바게트
ba gae teu
baguette

7 아이스크림
a i seu keu rim
ice cream

8 푸딩
pu ding
pudding

9 라자냐
la ja nya
lasagne

10 칠면조
chil myeon jo
turkey

11 애플파이
ae peul pa i
apple pie

12 햄
haem
ham

13 샐러드
sael leo deu
salad

15 스테이크
seu tae i keu
steak

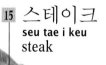

14 매시트
포테이토
maesiteu potaeito
mashed
potatoes

16 소시지
so si ji
sausage

17 서양식 아침
seoyangsik achim
Western breakfast

18 과일 쥬스
gwail juseu
fruit juice

19 커피
keo pi
coffee

20 베이컨;
훈제 햄
bae i keon;
hunjae
haem
bacon;
smoked
ham

21 한쪽 덜익은
계란
hanjjok deolikeun
gyaeran
sunny-side up eggs

22 토스트
to seu teu
toast

한국의 인기있는 패스트 푸드 체인
Hangug-ui ingiissneun paeseuteu pudeu chein
Some popular fast food chains in Korea

스타벅스 커피
seuta beokseu
kape
Starbucks

맥도날드
maekdonaldeu
McDonald's

케이에프씨
kaeiepeussi
KFC

피자헛
pijaheot
Pizza Hut

서브웨이
seobeuweii
Subway

버거킹
beogeoking
Burger King

23 케이크
kae i keu
cake

24 치즈
chi jeu
cheese

25 시리얼
si ri eol
ccrcal

26 오트밀
oteumil
oatmeal

Additional Vocabulary

29 서양음식
seo yang eum sik
Western-style food

30 맛있는
mat it neun
tasty; delicious

31 바베큐
ba bae kyu
barbecue

32 굽다
gup da
to roast; to bake

33 팬케이크
paen kae i keu
pancakes

34 버터; 크림
beoteo; keurim
butter; cream

35 요구르트
yo gu reu teu
yogurt

36 케찹/토마토
소스
kaechap/tomato soseu
ketchup;
tomato sauce

37 맥도날드는 한국에서 유명한 페스트푸드 음식점입니다.
Maekdonaldeuneun hankunaeseo yumyeonghan paeseuteupudeu eumsikjeomimnida.
McDonalds is a popular fast food restaurant in Korea.

38 모든 아이들은 햄버거와 감자튀김을 좋아합니다.
Modeun aideuleun haembeogeowa gamjatwigimeul joahapnida.
All children like hamburgers and french fries.

39 한국음식 혹은 서양음식중 어느걸 좋아하세요?
Hankukeumsik hokeun seoyangeumjung eoneugeol joahasaeyo?
Do you prefer Korean food or Western food?

27 햄버거
haem beo geo
hamburger

28 감자 튀김
gamja twigim
french fries

음료수
Eum ryo su
36 Drinks

1 음료
eum ryo
beverage

2 생수
saeng su
mineral water

3 과일 쥬스
gwail juseu
fruit juice

4 오렌지 쥬스
o raen ji jyu seu
orange juice

5 우유
u yu
milk

6 커피
keo pi
coffee

7 차
cha
tea

8 냉차
naeng cha
iced tea

9 두유
du yu
soy milk

10 콜라
kol la
cola

11 수돗물
su dot mul
tap water

12 물
mul
water

15 다이어트 음료수
da i eo teu eum ryo su
diet drinks

13 마시다
ma si da
to drink

14 목마른
mok ma reun
thirsty

16 에너지 음료
ae neo ji eum ryo
energy drinks

17 스포츠 음료
seu po cheu eum ryo
sports drinks

19 적포도주
jeok po do ju
red wine

20 백포도주
baek po do ju
white wine

18 칵테일
kak tae il
cocktails

21 위스키
wi seu ki
whiskey

22 샴페인
Syam pae in
Champagne

23 막걸리
mak geol li
rice wine

24 황주
hwang ju
yellow wine

25 소주
so ju
soju

26 맥주
maek ju
beer

Additional Vocabulary

27 탄산음료
tan san eum ryo
sodas

28 정수기
jeong su gi
water dispenser

29 뜨거운 물
ddeu geo un mul
hot water

30 찬 물
chan mul
cold water

31 얼음
eol eum
ice cubes

32 냉수
naeng su
ice water

33 유리; 컵
yuri; keop
glass; cup

34 병
byeong
bottle

35 매일 몇잔의 물을 마셔야하나요?
Maeil meotjanui muleul masyeoyahanayo?
How many glasses of water should people drink every day?

36 운전하면 음주하지마세요. 음주하면 운전하지마세요.
Unjeonhamyeon eumjuhajimasaeyo. Eumjuhamyeon unjeon-hajimasaeyo.
If you drive, don't drink. If you drink, don't drive.

37 따뜻한것을 마시고 싶어요.
Ddaeddeuthangeotseul masigo sipeoyo.
I want something hot to drink.

신선한 과일, 견과, 곡물

Sinseonhan gwail, gyeongwa, gokmul

Fieldsh Fruits, Nuts and Grains

37

1 사과
sagwa
apple

2 망고
manggo
mango

3 오렌지
oraenji
orange

4 귤
gyul
mandarin
orange

5 배
bae
pear

6 코코넛
kokoneot
coconut

7 바나나
banana
banana

8 파인애플
painaepeul
pineapple

9 복숭아
boksunga
peach

10 파파야
papaya
papaya

11 레몬
laemon
lemon

12 라임
laim
lime

13 자두
jadu
plums

14 참외
cham wei
yellow melon

15 딸기
ddalgi
strawberry

16 포도
podo
grapes

50 생과일 먹기를 좋아합니다.
Saenggwail meokgireul joahapnida.
I love to eat fresh fruits.

17 칸탈루프
kantallupeu
cantaloupe

18 감
gam
persimmon

19 수박
subak
watermelon

23 피스타치오
piseutachio
pistachios

20 땅콩
ddangkong
peanuts

21 호두
hodu
walnuts

22 피칸
pikan
pecans

24 아몬드
amondeu
almonds

29 캐슈넛
kaesyuneot
cashew nuts

25 마카다미아 넛
makadamia neot
macadamia nuts

26 밤
bam
chestnuts

27 헤이즐넛
haeijeulneot
hazel nuts

28 잣
jat
pine nuts

Additional Vocabulary

40 곡물
gokmul
cereals; grains

41 견과
gyeongwa
nuts

42 크래커
keuraekeo
crackers

43 오트밀
oteumil
oatmeal

44 건과
geongwa
dried fruits

45 콩
kong
beans

46 옥수수
oksusu
corn

47 밀가루
milgaru
flour

48 주스
juseu
juice

49 알레르기
allaereugi
allergy

30 호박씨
hobakssi
pumpkin seeds

31 수박씨
subakssi
watermelon seeds

32 해바라기씨
haebaragissi
sunflower seeds

33 참깨
chamggae
sesame seeds

34 오트
oteu
oats

35 보리
bori
barley

36 수수
susu
millet

37 메밀
maemil
buckwheat

38 쌀
ssal
rice

39 밀
mil
wheat

51 견과없이 샐러드 하나더
Gyeongwaeopsi saelleodeu hanadeo
줄수있나요?
julsuitnayo?
Can I have a salad without nuts?

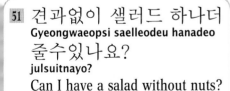

52 무슨 견과일을 좋아하세요?
Museun gyeongwaileul joahasaeyo?
What nuts do you like?

53 캐슈를 좋아해요. 당신은요?
Kaesyureul joahaeyo. Dangsineunyo?
I like cashew nuts. What about you?

54 견과에 알레르기가 있어요.
Gyeongwaae allaereugiga itsseoyo.
I am allergic to nuts.

81

38

시장에서
Sijangaeseo
At the Market

1 고기
go gi
meat

2 소고기
so go gi
beef

3 양고기
yang go gi
lamb; mutton

4 파슬리
pa seul li
parsley

5 돼지고기
dwei ji go gi
pork

6 코리앤더;
koriaendeo;
실란트로
sillanteuro
coriander
leaves;
cilantro

7 로즈메리
ro jeu mae ri
rosemary

8 오리고기
o ri go gi
duck

9 닭고기
dak go gi
chicken

10 레몬
laemon
lemon

11 해산물
hae san mul
seafood

12 문어
mun eo
octopus

13 딜
dil
dill

14 새우
sae u
shrimp;
prawns

15 물고기
mul go gi
fish

16 계란
gyae ran
eggs

17 야채
ya chae
vegetables

18 깻잎
kkaennip
perilla leaves

19 쑥갓
ssukgat
chrysanthemum
greens

20 옥수수
oksusu
corn

21 시금치
si geum chi
spinach

22 콩나물
kong na mul
bean sprouts

54 한국에서는 동네 마켓에서 음식사는걸 좋아해요.
Hankukaeseoneun dongnae makaetaeseo eumsiksaneungeol joahaeyo.
In Korea, we like to buy our food at the local market.

55 야채와 고기가 매우 신선해요. 그리고 수퍼마켓보다 약간 싸요.
Yachaewa gogiga maeu sinseonhaeyo. Geurigo supeomakaetboda yakgan ssayo.
The vegetables and meat are very fresh there. And it is slightly cheaper than the supermarket.

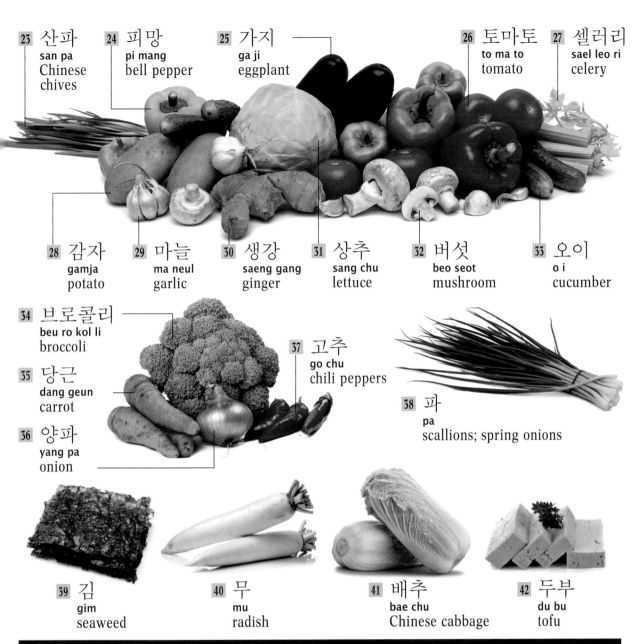

23 산파
san pa
Chinese chives

24 피망
pi mang
bell pepper

25 가지
ga ji
eggplant

26 토마토
to ma to
tomato

27 셀러리
sael leo ri
celery

28 감자
gamja
potato

29 마늘
ma neul
garlic

30 생강
saeng gang
ginger

31 상추
sang chu
lettuce

32 버섯
beo seot
mushroom

33 오이
o i
cucumber

34 브로콜리
beu ro kol li
broccoli

35 당근
dang geun
carrot

36 양파
yang pa
onion

37 고추
go chu
chili peppers

38 파
pa
scallions; spring onions

39 김
gim
seaweed

40 무
mu
radish

41 배추
bae chu
Chinese cabbage

42 두부
du bu
tofu

Additional Vocabulary

43 시장
si jang
market

44 식료품
sik ryo pum
groceries

45 식초
sik cho
vinegar

46 호박
ho bak
pumpkin

47 아스파라거스
aseuparageoseu
asparagus

48 주키니
ju ki ni
zucchini

49 바질
ba jil
basil

50 허브
heo beu
herb

51 간 쇠고기
gan swei go gi
ground/minced beef

52 간 돼지고기
gan dwei ji go gi
ground/minced pork

53 신선한
sin seon han
fresh

56 양념
yangnyeom
seasonings

57 간장
kanjang
soy sauce

58 멸치액젓
myulchiaekjeot
fermented
anchovy sauce

59 참기름
cham gi reum
sesame oil

60 올리브유
ollibeuyu
olive oil

61 고추장
gochujang
hot pepper paste

62 고추가루
gochukaroo
red chili powder

63 후추
hu chu
ground pepper

64 소금
sohkeum
salt

65 꿀
ggul
honey

66 된장
doenjang
soy bean paste

Additional Vocabulary

67 겨자
gyeoja
yellow mustard

68 설탕; 사탕
seoltang; satang
sugar; candy

69 미린
milin
rice wine

70 새우젓
saeujeot
fermented shrimp

71 진간장
jin kanjang
dark soy sauce

72 녹말
nogmal
starch

73 조청
jochung
rice malt syrup

74 콩기름
kongireum
soy bean oil

75 식용유
shik yong yu
vegetable oil

76 먼저 재료를 준비하고 요리를 시작합니다.
Meonjeo jaelyoleul junbihago yolileul sijaghabnida.
First we'll prepare the ingredients, and then we'll start to cook.

77 그녀의 요리는 단순 할뿐만 아니라 맛있습니다.
Geunyeoui yolineun dansun halppunman anila mas-issseubnida.
Her dishes are not only simple, but also delicious.

84

English-Korean Index

corn 옥수수 **oksusu** [37-46] *81;* [38-20] *82*

cosmetics 화장품 **hwajang- pum** [10-17] *27*

country code 나라 번호 **nara beonho** [24-32] *54*

Countries in Southeast Asia 동남아시아 **Dongnam a si a** [32-1] *70*

course 과목 **gwamok** [21-22] *49*

cousin 조카 **jo ka** [2-28] *10*

cousins 사촌 **sa chon** [2-29] *10*

cow 소 **so** [29-16] *65*

crackers 크래커 **keuraekeo** [37-42] *81*

credit card 신용카드 **sin yong ka deu** [9-14] *25;* [10-30] *27*

crops 농작물 **nong jak mul** [17-17] *41*

cucumber 오이 **o i** [38-33] *83*

culture 문화 **munhwa** [21-17] *49*

currency 통화 **tong hwa** [31-20] *69*

currency exchange 외화환전 **weihwa hwanjeon** [9-16] *25*

curtain 커튼 **keo teun** [3-17] *12*

D

dad 아빠 **a ppa** [2-37] *10*

Dano Festival 단오축제 **dano chukjae** [18-32] *43*

dance (performance art) 무용 **mu yong** [26-21] *59*

dark color 어두운색 **eoduun saek** [7-15] *20*

dark soy sauce 진간장 **jin kanjang** [38-71] *84*

daughter 딸 **ddal** [2-5] *10*

day 일 **il** [16-3] *38*

day of a month 날짜 **nal jja** [16-36] *39*

decade (10 years) 10년 **sip nyeon** [16-37] *39*

December 십이월 **sip i wal** [16-27] *39*

decision 결정 **gyeoljeong** [10-36] *27*

debt 부채 **bu chae** [9-25] *25*

deer 사슴 **sa seum** [29-8] *64*

dentistry 치과 **chigwa** [27-22] *61*

depart 출발 **chul bal** [8-21] *23*

department store 백화점 **baekhwajeom** [10-23] *27*

delivery van 배달용밴 **baedalyong baen** [12-7] *30*

dentist 치과의사 **chi gwa ui sa** [25-14] *57*

deposit 예금 **yea geum** [9-26] *25*

dermatology 피부과 **pibugwa** [27-29] *61*

desk 책상 **chaek sang** [3-36] *13*

diary 일기 **il gi** [16-44] *39;* **il gi** [31-22] *69*

dictionary 사전 **sa jeon** [19-11] *44*

diet drinks 다이어트음료수 **da i eo teu eum ryo su** [36-15] *78*

difficult 어려운 **eoryeoun** [8-16] *23;* [21-28] *49*

digestion 소화 **so hwa** [4-37] *15*

digits 자릿수 **jaritsu** [5-29] *17*

dill 딜 **dil** [38-13] *82*

dining table 저녁 식탁 **jeonyeok siktak** [6-31] *18*

dish of steamed rice, vegetables, egg and mea 비빔밥 **bi bim bap** [34-16] *75*

distance 거리 **geori** [13-37] *33*

direction 방향 **banghyang** [13-36] *33*

discount 할인 **hal in** [9-20] *25*

do not have 없다 **eop da** [8-17] *23*

doctor 의사 **ui sa** [27-4] *60*

doctor's consultation room 상담실 **sangdamshil** [27-18] *60*

dog 개 **gae** [29-25] *65*

donuts 도너츠 **do neo cheu** [35-5] *76*

door 문 **mun** [3-46] *13*

down 아래 **a rae** [8-1] *22*

dragon 용 **yong** [29-23] *65*

drawer 서랍 **seo rap** [3-32] *13*

dried fruits 건과 **geongwa** [37-44] *81*

drive a car 차를운전하다 **chareul unjeonhada** [12-24] *31*

driver 운전사 **un jeon sa** [12-3] *30*

drum 북 **buk** [26-5] *58*

dry 마른 **ma reun** [8-8] *22*

duck 오리 **o ri** [29-9] *64*

duck 오리고기 **o ri go gi** [38-8] *82*

dumplings 만두 **man du** [34-18] *75*

E

ear 귀 **gwi** [4-2] *14*

ear, nose and throat 이빈후과 **i bin hu gwa** [27-25] *61*

early 일찍 **il jjik** [15-24] *37*

early morning 이른 아침 **il reun a chim** [15-18] *37*

earth; ground 지구; 땅 **ji gu; ddang** [28-31] *63*

east 동 **dong** [13-10] *32*

East Timor 동티모르 **Dong ti mo reu** [32-12] *70*

Easter 부활절 **bu hwal jeol** [18-18] *43*

easy 쉬운 **swiun** [8-16] *23;* [21-27] *49*

eat till full 배부른 **bae bu reun** [8-20] *23*

eggplant 가지 **ga ji** [38-25] *83*

eggs 계란 **gyae ran** [38-16] *82*

eight 여덟 **yeodeol** [5-8] *16*

eight pieces of clothing 옷여덟벌 **ot yeodeolbeol** [22-5] *50*

elbow 팔꿈치 **pal ggum chi** [4-20] *15*

electric car 전동차 **jeon dong cha** [28-6] *62*

electric socket; power point 전기 소켓 **jeongi sokaet** [3-50] *12*

elementary school 초등학 **cho deung hak gyo** [20-27] *47*

elephant 코끼리 **ko kki ri** [29-17] *65*

elevator 승강기 **seung gang gi** [3-45] *13*

email 이메일 **i mae il** [23-15] *52*

embassy 대사관 **dae sa gwan** [31-28] *69*

emergency 비상 **bi sang** [27-39] *61*

emergency room 응급실 **ueng geup shil** [27-2] *60*

employee 직원 **jik won** [25-26] *57*

employment 고용 **go yong** [25-30] *57*

end 끝 **ggeut** [8-24] *23*

engineer 기술자 **gi sul ja** [25-4] *56*

English 영어 **yeong eo** [19-38] *45;* [33-1] *64*

enter 들어가다 **deul-eogada** [8-6] *22*

energy drinks 에너지음료 **ae neo ji eum ryo** [36-16] *78*

environment 환경 **hwan gyeong** [28-28] *63*

equals 같은 **gateun** [5-21] *17*

eraser 지우개 **ji u gae** [19-15] *45*

essay 에세이 **aesaei** [21-16] *49*

Europe 유럽 **Yu reop** [32-16] *71*

eye 눈 **nun** [4-8] *14*

eyebrow 눈썹 **nun sseop** [4-7] *14*

even numbers 짝수 **jjaksu** [5-25] *17*

exam 시험 **si heom** [19-1] *44*

exercise book 연습장 **yeonseupjang** [21-24] *49*

exit 출구 **chul gu** [8-6] *22*

expensive 비싼 **bi ssan** [9-22] *25*

expressway 고속도로 **go sok do ro** [11-18] *29*

F

face 얼굴 **eol gul** [4-5] *14*

Facebook 페이스북 **pae i seu bok** [24-18] *55*

fake 가짜 **ga jja** [8-27] *23*

family 가족 **ga jok** [2-30] *10*

fan 부채 **buchae** [17-14] *41*

far 먼 **meon** [8-25] *23;* [13-43] *33*

farmer 농부 **nong bu** [25-19] *57*

fast 빠른 **ppa reun** [8-28] *23*

fat 뚱뚱한 **ddungddunghan** [0-14] *23*

father 아버지 **abuh ji** [2-12] *11*

faucet 수도꼭지 **su do ggok ji** [3-39] *13*

February 이월 **i wal** [16-17] *39*

female 여자 **yeo ja** [2-3] *10*

fermented anchovy sauce 멸치액젓 **myulchiaekjeot** [38-58] *84*

fermented shrimp 새우젓 **saeujeot** [38-70] *84*

festival; holiday 축제, 휴일 **chukjae, hyuil** [18-1] *42*

fever 열 **yeol** [27-12] *60*

fifteen minutes past six 6시 15분 **yeoseotsi sipobun** [15-8] *36*

fifteen minutes to seven 7시 15분전 **ilgopsi simobunjeon** [15-10] *36*

file 파일 **pa il** [23-22] *53*

fingers 손가락 **son ga rak** [4-15] *14*

fingernails 손톱 **son top** [4-43] *15*

finishing line 결승선 **gyeol seung seon** [30-14] *67*

fire engine 소방차 **so bang cha** [12-16] *31*

fireworks 불꽃놀이 **bul ggot nol i** [18-3] *42*

first aid kit 구급상자 **gugeub sangja** [27-50] *61*

first birthday 돌 **dol** [18-6] *42*

First we'll prepare the ingredients, and then we'll start to cook. 먼저재료를준비하고요리를시작합니다. **Meonjeo jaelyoleul junbihago yolileul sijaghabnida.** [38-76] *84*

fish 물고기 **mul go gi** [29-31] *65;* [38-15] *82*

five 다섯 **daseot** [5-5] *16*

five minutes past six 6시5분 **yeoseotsi o bun** [15-5] *36*

five minutes to seven 7시5분전 **ilgopsi obunjeon** [15-11] *36*

five tickets 표다섯장 **pyo da seot jang** [22-4] *50*

flash cards 플래시카드 **peullaesi kadeu** [21-7] *49*

floor 바닥 **ba da** [3-14] *12*

flour 밀가루 **milgaru** [37-47] *81*

flower 꽃 **ggot** [28-2] *62*

flower pot 화분 **hwa bun** [28-25] *63*

fog 안개 **an gae** [14-24] *35*

foot 발 **bal** [4-23] *15*; 피트 **piteu** [13-41] *33*

forehead 이마 **i ma** [4-17] *15*

foreign language 외국어 **wui kuk eo** [19-43] *45*

foreigner 외국인 **wei kuk in** [31-10] *68*

forest 숲 **sup** [28-13] *63*

fork 포크 **po keu** [34-13] *74*

four 넷 **naet** [5-4] *16*

four seasons 사계절 **sa gyae jeol** [17-19] *41*

four-story building 사층건물 **sacheung geonmul** [22-11] *51*

fraction 분수 **bunsu** [5-24] *17*

French 프랑스어 **Peu rang seu eo** [33-2] *64*

french fries 감자튀김 **gamja twigim** [35-28] *77*

frequently 자주 **ja ju** [15-33] *37*

fresh 신선한 **sin seon han** [38-53] *83*

freshman 대학1학년 **daehak ilhaknyeon** [20-34] *47*

Friday 금요일 **geum yo il** [16-14] *38*

friend 친구 **chin gu** [1-13] *8*

frog 개구리 **gae gu ri** [29-12] *64*

from 부터 **buteo** [27-43] *61*

fruit juice 과일쥬스 **gwail juseu** [35-18] *77*; [36-3] *78*

future 미래 **mi rae** [8-23] *23*

G

garage 차고 **cha go** [3-56] *12*

garbage truck 쓰레기차 **sseu rae gi cha** [12-6] *30*

garden 정원 **jeong won** [28-1] *62*

garlic 마늘 **ma neul** [38-29] *83*

gas station; petrol statio 주유소 **ju yu so** [11-6] *28*

gathering; meeting 모임 **mo im** [1-19] *9*

general medicine 내과 **naegwa** [27-23] *61*

general surgery 외과 **wuigwa** [27-24] *61*

generally 일반적으로 **ilbanjeokeuro** [10-34] *27*

German 독일어 **Dok il eo** [33-4] *64*

gift 선물 **seon mul** [18-20] *43*

ginger 생강 **saeng gang** [38-30] *83*

ginseng 인삼 **in sam** [34-30] *75*

ginseng chicken soup 삼계탕 **samgyetang** [34-19] *75*

giraffe 기린 **gilin** [29-3] *64*

girl's older brother 오빠 **o ppa** [2-17] *11*

girl's older sister 언니 **un ni** [2-16] *11*

give 주다 **ju da** [8-2] *22*

giving directions 방향알려주기 **banghyang alryeojugi** [13-21] *32*

glass; cup 유리; 컵 **yuri; keop** [36-33] *79*

glasses; spectacles 안경 **angyeong** [10-11] *26*

globe 지구 **ji gu** [32-28] *71*

gloves 장갑 **jang gap** [14-30] *35*

Gmarket 지마켓 **ji ma kaet** [24-16] *55*

go 가다 **ga da** [8-18] *23*

go faster 빨리가다 **bbal li ga da** [12-27] *31*

go straight 똑바로가다 **ddok ba ro ga da** [12-29] *31*; 직진 **jikjin** [13-31] *33*

go to school 등교하다 **deung gyo ha da** [6-25] *18*

go to work/get off work 출근하다/퇴근하다 **chulgeunhada/tweigeunhada** [6-24] *18*

goat 염소 **yeomso** [29-14] *65*

going to work 출근 **chul geun** [25-23] *57*

gold 금색 **geum saek** [7-13] *20*

golf 골프 **gol peu** [30-15] *67*

good 좋은 **jo eun** [8-7] *22*

good weather 좋은날씨 **jo eun nalssi** [14-33] *35*

Google 구글 **gu geul** [24-19] *55*

grade; class 학년 **hak nyeon** [19-23] *45*

grades 성적 **seong jeok** [20-22] *47*

grammar 문법 **munbeop** [21-18] *49*

grandson 손자 **son ja** [2-27] *10*

grapes 포도 **podo** [37-16] *80*

grass 풀 **pul** [28-5] *62*

gray 회색 **hwei saek** [7-10] *20*

Greek 그리스어 **Geu ri seu eo** [33-10] *65*

green 녹색 **nok saek** [7-7] *20*

green onion pancake 파전 **pajeon** [34-28] *75*

groceries 식료품 **sik ryo pum** [38-44] *83*

ground/minced beef 간쇠고기 **gan swei go gi** [38-51] *83*

ground/minced pork 간돼지고기 **gan dwei ji go gi** [38-52] *83*

ground pepper 후추 **hu chu** [38-63] *84*

guest; customer 손님 **son nim** [1-20] *9*

guitar 기타 **gi ta** [26-1] *58*

gym 헬스장 **hael seu jang** [11-19] *29*

gynecology 산부인과 **san bu in gwa** [27-27] *61*

H

hail 우박 **u bak** [14-28] *35*

hair 머리카락 **meo ri ka rak** [4-6] *14*

half past six 6시30 **yeoseotsi samsipbun** [15-9] *36*

Halloween 할로윈 **hal lo win** [18-17] *43*

ham 햄 **haem** [35-12] *76*

hamburger 햄버거 **haem beo geo** [35-27] *77*

hand 손 **son** [4-18] *15*

Hangame 한게임 **han gae im** [24-20] *55*

happy 행복 **haengbok** [1-10] *8*

Happy birthday! 생일축하합니다! **Saengil chukhahapnida!** [18-34] *43*

harbor 항구 **hang gu** [28-18] *63*

harp 하프 **hapeu** [26-2] *58*

hat 모자 **moja** [10-16] *26*; [14-29] *35*

have 있다 **it da** [8-17] *23*

hazel nuts 헤이즐넛 **haei-jeulneot** [37-27] *81*

head 머리 **meo ri** [4-1] *14*

health 건강 **geon gang** [4-47] *15*

healthy 건강 **geon gang** [30-28] *67*

heart 심장 **sim jang** [4-32] *15*

Hebrew 히브리어 **Hi beu ri eo** [33-11] *65*

hello (on the phone) 여보세요 **yeobo seyo** [1-36] *9*

here 여기 **yeogi** [13-2] *32*

herb 허브 **heo beu** [38-50] *83*

high speed train 고속열차 **go sok yeol cha** [12-8] *30*

Hindi 힌두어 **Hin du eo** [33-13] *65*

history 역사 **yeok sa** [19-30] *45*

home delivery 집배원 **jipbaewon** [10-27] *27*

homework 숙제 **suk jae** [19-28] *45*

honey 꿀 **ggul** [38-65] *84*

honeymoon 신혼여행 **sin hon yeo haeng** [31-18] *69*

horse 말 **mal** [29-18] *65*

hospital 병원 **byeong won** [27-1] *60*

hot 더운 **deo un** [14-19] *35*

hot dog 핫도그 **hat do geu** [35-1] *76*

hot pepper paste 고추장 **gochujang** [38-61] *84*

hot water 뜨거운물 **ddeu geo un mul** [36-29] *79*

hot weather 더운날씨 **deo un nalssi** [14-20] *35*

hotel 호텔 **ho tael** [11-1] *28*; [31-1] *68*

hour 시간 **si gan** [15-1] *36*

house 집 **jip** [3-51] *12*

housefly 파리 **pa ri** [29-28] *65*

How much longer? 얼마나 더? **Eolmana deo?** [13-56] *33*

hungry 배고픈 **bae go peun** [8-20] *23*

hurricane 허리케인 **heori-kaein** [14-37] *35*

hurts 아파 **apa** [27-40] *61*

husband 남편 **nam pyeon** [2-24] *10*

husband and wife 부부 **bu bu** [2-13] *11*

I

I; me 나 **na** [2-18] *11*

ice cream 아이스크림 **a i seu keu rim** [35-7] *76*

ice cubes 얼음 **eol eum** [36-31] *79*

ice water 냉수 **naeng su** [36-32] *79*

ice-skating 아이스케이팅 **a i seu kayiting** [30-16] *67*

iced tea 냉차 **naeng cha** [36-8] *78*

idiom 숙어 **sukeo** [21-11] *49*

immediately 즉시 **jeuksi** [13-57] *33*

in a moment 금방 **geum hang** [15-34] *37*

in front 앞 **ap** [13-14] *32*

in the afternoon; p.m. 오후 **o hu** [15-21] *37*

in the morning; a.m. 아침,오전 **a chim, o jeon** [15-19] *37*

Independence Day 광복절 **gwang bok jeol** [18-19] *43*

India 인도 **In do** [32-25] *71*

Indonesia 인도네시아 **In do nae si a** [32-11] *70*

Indonesian 인도네시아어 **In do ne si a eo** [33-14] *65*

injection 주사 **jusa** [27-17] *60*

inside 안 **an** [8-22] *23*; [13-34] *33*

instrument 악기 **ak gi** [26-30] *59*

intelligent; clever 현명한; 똑똑한 **hyeonmyeonghan; ddokddokhan** [20-23] *47*

Internet 인터넷 **inteonaet** [23-28] 53

Internet cafes 인터넷 카페 **inteonaet kapae** [24-4] 54

Internet language 인터넷언어 **inteonaet eoneo** [24-26] 54

Internet slang 인터넷은어 **inteonaet euneo** [24-28] 54

intestines 장 **jang** [4-34] 15

introduce yourself 자신을 소개하다 **jasineul sogaehada** [1-14] 9

island 섬 **seom** [31-24] 69

Italian 이탈어 **I tal i eo** [33-5] 64

Italy 이탈리 **Il tal li** [32-27] 71

J

January 일월 **il wal** [16-16] 39

Japan 일본 **Il bon** [32-21] 71

Japanese 일본어 **Il bon eo** [33-8] 64

jazz 재즈 **jae jeu** [26-28] 59

jeans 청바지 **cheongbaji** [10-9] 26

joyful 즐거운 **jeul geo un** [1-11] 8

journal 일기 **il gi** [31-22] 69

judge 판사 **pan sa** [25-2] 56

juice 주스 **juseu** [37-48] 81

July 칠월 **chil wal** [16-22] 39

June 유월 **yu wal** [16-21] 39

junior year in college 대학 3 학년 **daehak samhaknyeon** [20-36] 47

junior year of high school 고 등학교 3 학년 **godeunghak-gyo sam haknyeon** [20-31] 47

K

Kakao Talk 카카오토크 **kakaotokeu** [24-6] 54

karaoke 가라오케 **ga ra o kae** [26-11] 59

ketchup; tomato sauce 케챱/토마토소스 **kaechap/tomato soseu** [35-36] 77

kettle 주전자 **ju jeon ja** [3-29] 13

keyboard 키보드 **ki bo deu** [23-5] 52

keys 열쇠 **yeol swei** [3-5] 12

kidneys 신장 **sin jang** [4-33] 15

kilometer 킬로미터 **killo-miteo** [13-38] 33

Kimchi 김치 **kim chi** [34-5] 74

kitchen 부엌 **bu eo** [3-23] 13

knee 무릎 **mu reup** [4-21] 15

knife 칼 **kal** [34-14] 74

knife-cut noodles 칼국수 **kal kuk su** [34-21] 75

Korea 한국 **Han kuk** [32-22] 71

Korean 한국말 **Han kuk mal** [33-16] 65

Korean character 한글 **hangeul** [21-4] 49

Korean language 한국 **hankukmal** [21-9] 49

Korean restaurant 한국식당 **hankuk sikdang** [34-1] 74

Korean zither-like string instrument 가야금 **gaya-geum** [26-8] 58

L

L size 라지 **la ji** [7-33] 21

laboratory 실험실 **sil heom sil** [20-20] 47

laboratory test 실험실검사 **shilheomshil geomsa** [27-8] 60

lamb; mutton 양고기 **yang go gi** [38-3] 82

lasagne 라자냐 **la ja nya** [35-9] 76

lake 호수 **ho su** [31-12] 68

Laos 라오스 **La o seu** [32-6] 70

laptop 노트북 **no teu buk** [23-6] 52

large 라지 **la ji** [7-35] 21

larger 더큰 **deo keun** [7-41] 21

last month 전달 **jeon dal** [16-41] 39

last week 지난주 **ji na ju** [16-40] 39

last year 작년 **jak nyeon** [16-28] 39

lawyer 변호사 **byeon ho sa** [25-1] 56

leaf 나뭇잎 **na mut ip** [28-29] 63

leap year 윤년 **yun nyeon** [16-35] 39

lecture hall 강의실 **gang ui sil** [20-14] 46

left side 왼쪽 **wenjjok** [13-29] 33

leg 다리 **da ri** [4-22] 15

leisure 여가 **yeo ga** [6-34] 18

lemon 레몬 **laemon** [37-11] 80; [38-10] 82

less 적은 **jeok eun** [8-3] 22

lesson 수업 **sueop** [21-21] 49

letter 편지 **pyeon ji** [19-12] 44

lettuce 상추 **sang chu** [38-31] 83

level (of achievement) 수준 **su jun** [19-48] 45

library 도서관 **do seo gwan** [11-22] 29; [20-3] 46

light color 밝은색 **balgeun saek** [7-16] 20

light switch 전등 스위치 **jeondeung seuweichi** [3-49] 12

lightning 번개 **beon gae** [14-11] 34

lime 라임 **laim** [37-12] 80

linguistics 언어학 **eoneohak** [21-20] 49

lion 사자 **sa ja** [29-5] 64

lip 입술 **ip sul** [4-14] 14

literature 문학 **mun hak** [19-29] 45

liver 간 **gan** [4-35] 15

living room 거실 **geo sil** [3-1] 12

loan 융자 **yung ja** [9-24] 25

long 긴 **gin** [8-10] 22

long distance call 징기리통화 **janggeori tonghwa** [24-31] 54

long-distance running 먼거리달리기 **meongeori dal li gi** [30-10] 66

love 사랑 **sa rang** [19-34] 45

luggage 짐 **jim** [31-4] 68

Lunar New Year 음력새해 **eumryeok saehae** [18-10] 42

Lunar New Year's Eve 음력새해전야 **eumryeok saehae jeonya** [18-9] 42

lungs 폐 **pae** [4-31] 15

M

M size 미디엄 **mi di eom** [7-30] 21

macadamia nuts 마카다미아넛 **makadamia neot** [37-25] 81

magazine 잡지 **jap ji** [19-10] 44

magpie 까치 **kka chi** [29-21] 65

Malaysia 말레이시아 **Mal lae i si a** [32-8] 70

male 남자 **nam ja** [2-2] 10

manager 부장 **bu jang** [25-16] 56

Mandarin Chinese 중국어 **Jung kuk eo** [33-19] 65

mandarin orange 귤 **gyul** [37-4] 80

mango 망고 **manggo** [37-2] 80

map 지도 **ji do** [31-2] 68

March 삼월 **sam wal** [16-18] 39

marinated grilled meat 불고기 **bulgogi** [34-24] 75

market 시장 **si jang** [38-43] 83

mashed potatoes 매시트포테이토 **maesiteu potaeito** [35-14] 76

maternal grandfather 외할아버지 **oe hal abuh ji** [2-9] 11

maternal grandmother 외할머니 **oe hal muh ni** [2-10] 11

mathematics 수학 **su hak** [19-4] 44

May 오월 **o wal** [16-20] 39

meat 고기 **go gi** [38-1] 82

medicine 약 **yak** [27-15] 60

medium 미디엄 **mi di eom** [7-36] 21

menu 메뉴 **mae nyu** [34-4] 74

meter 미터 **miteo** [13-40] 33

Microsoft 마이크로소프트 **maikeurosopeuteu** [24-23] 55

microwave oven 전자레인지 **jeonjaraeinji** [3-24] 13

middle; center 중간 **junggan** [13-28] 33

middle school 중학교 **jung hak gyo** [20-28] 47

midnight 자정 **ja jeong** [15-22] 37

mile 마일 **mail** [13-39] 33

milk 우유 **u yu** [36-5] 78

millennium (1000 years) 천년 **cheon nyeon** [16-39] 39

millet 수수 **susu** [37-36] 81

mineral water 생수 **saeng su** [36-2] 78

minute 분 **bun** [15-2] 36

mobile phone 휴대폰 **hyu dae pon** [24-9] 54

mother 어머니 **uh muh ni** [2-14] 11

mom 엄마 **um ma** [2-38] 10

Monday 월요일 **wal yo il** [16-10] 38

monkey 원숭이 **won sung i** [29-6] 64

month 월 **wal** [16-2] 38

monument 기념물 **gi nyeom mul** [11-31] 29; [31-33] 69

moon 달 **dal** [14-26] 35

more 많은 **man eun** [8-3] 22

more; even more 더; 훨씬 더 **deo; hweolssin deo** [10-35] 27

mosquito 모기 **mo gi** [29-27] 65

motorcycle 오토바이 **o to ba i** [12-9] 30

mountain climbing 등산 **deung san** [30-4] 66

mouse 마우스 **ma u seu** [23-10] 52; [29-13] 64

mousepad 마우스패드 **mauseu paedeu** [23-9] 52

mouth 입 **ip** [4-10] 14

multimedia 멀티미디어 **meol ti mi di eo** [23-34] 53 muscles 근육 **geun yuk** [4-25] 15

museum 박물관 **bak mul gwan** [11-10] 28; [31-31] 69

mushroom 버섯 **beo seot** [38-32] 83

music 음악 **eum ak** [19-39] 45; [26-20] 59

musical performance 음악공연 **eumak gongyeon** [26-26] 59

musician 음악가 **eum ak ga** [25-8] 56

Myanmar 미얀마 **Mi yan ma** [32-3] 70

N

name 이름 **i reum** [1-23] *9*

nationality 국적 **kuk jeok** [1-27] *9*

natural gas 천연 가스 **cheon yeon ga seu** [28-15] *63*

navel 배꼽 **bae ggop** [4-36] *15*

Naver 네이버 **nae i beo** [24-17] *55*

near 가까운 **ga gga un** [8-25] *23*; 근처 **geuncheo** [13-42] *33*

nearby 근처 **geuncheo** [13-50] *33*

neck 목 **mok** [4-3] *14*

necktie 넥타이 **naektai** [10-15] *26*

neighbor 이웃 **i ut** [11-28] *29*

nephew 조카 **jo ka** [2-21] *11*

network; Internet 네트워크; 인터넷 **naeteuwokeu; inteonaet** [24-25] *54*

network card 네트워크카드 **naeteuweokeu kadeu** [23-33] *53*

networking 네트워킹 **naeteuwoking** [23-24] *53*

neurology 신경학 **sin kyeong hak** [27-32] *61*

new 새것 **sae geot** [8-4] *22*

New Year 새해 **sae hae** [18-2] *42*

New Year's Day 새해첫날 **saehae cheotnal** [18-4] *42*

newspaper 신문 **sin mun** [19-9] *44*

next month 다음달 **da eum dal** [16-43] *39*

next week 다음주 **da eum ju** [16-42] *39*

next year 다음해 **daeumhae** [16-31] *39*

niece 조카딸 **jokattal** [2-22] *11*

night 밤 **bam** [15-16] *37*

night class 야간수업 **yagan sueop** [20-38] *47*

nine 아홉 **ahop** [5-9] *16*

no 아니요 **a ni yo** [8-19] *23*

noon 정오 **jeong o** [15-20] *37*

north 북 **buk** [13-6] *32*

North America 북아메리카 **Bukamaerika** [32-14] *71*

northeast 북동 **bukdong** [13-8] *32*

northwest 북서 **bukseo** [13-7] *32*

nose 코 **ko** [4-9] *14*

notebook 노트북 **no teu buk** [19-19] *45*

November 십일월 **sip il wal** [16-26] *39*

nuclear energy 원자력 **won ja ryeok** [28-16] *63*

numbers 숫자 **sutja** [5-28] *17*

nurse 간호사 **gan ho sa** [25-6] *56*; [27-3] *60*

nuts 견과 **gyeongwa** [37-41] *81*

O

oatmeal 오트밀 **oteumil** [35-26] *77*; [37-43] *81*

oats 오트 **oteu** [37-34] *81*

ocean 바다 **ba da** [28-7] *62*

October 시월 **si wal** [16-25] *39*

octopus 문어 **mun eo** [38-12] *82*

odd numbers 홀수 **holsu** [5-26] *17*

office 사무실 **sa mu sil** [25-15] *56*

ointment 연고 **yeon go** [27-37] *61*

old 오래된 **o rae dwen** [8-4] *22*; 늙은 **neulgeun** [8-11] *23*

older daughter 큰딸 **keun ddal** [2-33] *10*

older son 큰아들 **keun a deul** [2-32] *10*

olive oil 올리브유 **ollibeuyu** [38-60] *84*

oncology 종양학 **jong yang hak** [27-30] *61*

one 하나 **hana** [5-1] *16*

one bowl of soup 국한그릇 **guk hangeureut** [22-6] *50*

one chair 의자한개 **uija hangae** [22-8] *50*

one group of people 사람한 그룹 **saram hangeurup** [22-9] *51*

one half 반 **ban** [5-11] *16*

one quarter 4분의1 **sabunuiil** [5-13] *16*

one side 한쪽 **hanjjok** [13-52] *33*

one third 3분의1 **sambunuiil** [5-14] *16*

onion 양파 **yang pa** [38-36] *83*

online 온라인 **onlain** [23-23] *53*

online friends 온라인 친구 들 **onlain chingudeul** [24-2] *54*

online search 온라인서치 **onlain sseochi** [23-41] *53*

online shopping 온라인쇼핑 **onlain syoping** [10-29] *27*; [24-3] *54*

open 열린 **yeol lin** [8-13] *23*

opera 오페라 **o pae ra** [26-15] *59*

operating system 운영체제 **unyeong chaejae** [23-20] *53*

ophthalmology 안과 **angwa** [27-28] *61*

opposite 반대 **bandae** [13-44] *33*

orange (colour) 오렌지색 **o raen ji saek** [7-11] *20*

orange (fruit) 오렌지 **oraenji** [37-3] *80*

orange juice 오렌지쥬스 **o raen ji jyu seu** [36-4] *78*

other 다른 **dareun** [10-37] *27*

outside 밖 **bak** [8-22] *23*; [13-33] *33*

oven 오븐 **o beun** [3-27] *13*

P

painting 그림 **geu rim** [3-6] *12*

pancakes 팬케이크 **paen kae i keu** [35-33] *77*

papaya 파파야 **papaya** [37-10] *80*

paper 종이 **jong i** [19-13] *45*

paper currency 지폐 **ji pyae** [9-2] *24*

Parent's Day 어버이날 **eobeoinal** [18-11] *42*

parents 부모님 **bu mo nim** [2-6] *10*

park 공원 **gong won** [28-3] *62*

parsley 파슬리 **pa seul li** [38-4] *82*

part time 아르바이트 **a reu ba i teu** [25-29] *57*

passenger 승객 **seung gaek** [12-19] *31*

passport 여권 **yeo gwon** [31-7] *68*

password 비밀번호 **bi mil beon ho** [23-17] *53*

past 과거 **gwa geo** [8-23] *23*; [15-32] *37*

pasta; spaghetti 파스타; 스 파게티 **pasueta; seupagaeti** [35-4] *76*

pastor 목사 **mok sa** [25-3] *56*

paternal grandfather 할아버 지 **hal abuh ji** [2-7] *11*

paternal grandmother 할머 니 **hal muh ni** [2-8] *11*

patient 환자 **hwan ja** [27-5] *60*

PC 피씨 **pi ssi** [23-4] *52*

peach 복숭아 **boksunga** [37-9] *80*

peach blossoms 복숭아꽃 **bok sung a ggot** [17-7] *40*

peanuts 땅콩 **ddangkong** [37-20] *81*

pear 배 **bae** [37-5] *80*

pecans 피칸 **pikan** [37-22] *81*

pedestrian 보행자 **bohaengja** [11-34] *29*

pedestrian crossing 횡단보 도 **hoengdan bodo** [11-35] *29*

pediatrics 소아과 **so a gwa** [27-26] *61*

pedicab; trishaw 삼륜자전거 **samryun jajeongeo** [12-18] *31*

pen 펜 **paen** [19-14] *45*

pencil 연필 **yeon pil** [19-21] *45*

pencil case 필통 **pil tong** [19-35] *45*

pencil sharpener 연필깎기 **yeonpil kkakkgi** [19-17] *45*

percent (%) 퍼센트 **peos-aenteu** [5-23] *17*

performance 공연 **gong yeon** [26-22] *59*

performer 연기자 **yeon gi ja** [26-18] *59*

perilla leaves 깻잎 **kkaennip** [38-18] *82*

persimmon 감 **gam** [37-18] *80*

pertaining to 에관한 **e gwan-han** [27-49] *61*

Philippines 필리핀 **Pil li pin** [32-5] *70*

phone cards 전화카드 **jeonhwakadeu** [24-30] *54*

phone charger 전화충전기 **jeonhwa chungjeongi** [24-29] *54*

photocopier 복사기 **bok sa gi** [20-7] *46*

photograph 사진 **sa jin** [31-14] *68*

phrase 구절 **gujeol** [21-14] *49*

physical education 체육 **chae yuk** [19-5] *44*

physiotherapy 물리치료 **mul li chi ryo** [27-31] *61*

physics 물리학 **mul ri hak** [19-40] *45*

piano 피아노 **piano** [26-9] *58*

picnic 소풍 **so pung** [31-19] *69*

pigeon 비둘기 **bi dul gi** [29-20] *65*

pillow 베개 **bae gae** [3-19] *12*

pills 알약 **al yak** [27-16] *60*

PIN code 핀코드 **pin kodeu** [23-38] *53*

pineapple 파인애플 **pain-aepeul** [37-8] *80*

pine nuts 잣 **jat** [37-28] *81*

pink 분홍색 **bun hong saek** [7-12] *20*

pistachios 피스타치오 **piseutachio** [37-23] *81*

pizza 피자 **pi ja** [35-3] *76*

place 장소 **jangso** [13-51] *33*

plate 접시 **jeop si** [34-12] *74*

play basketball 농구하다 **nong gu hada** [30-24] *67*

plums 자두 **jadu** [37-13] *80*

poem 시 **si** [21-15] *49*

police officer 경찰관 **gyeong chal gwan** [25-21] *57*

police station 경찰서 **gyeong chal seo** [11-17] *29*

pollution 오염 **o yeom** [28-4] *62*

pool 수영장 **su yeong jang** [31-16] *69*

pop culture 대중문화 **daejung munhwa** [26-31] *59*

pop music 대중 음악 **dae jung eum ak** [26-24] *59*

pork 돼지고기 **dwei ji go gi** [38-5] *82*

ports 포트 **po teu** [23-14] *52*

Portuguese 포르투갈어 **Po reu tu gal eo** [33-18] *65*

postcard 엽서 **yeop seo** [31-29] *69*

potato 감자 **gamja** [38-28] *83*

potted plant 화분식 **hwabun sikmul** [3-47] *13*

post office 우체국 **u chae kuk** [11-16] *29*

practice 연습 **yeonseup** [21-23] *49*

prescription 처방 **cheo bang** [27-35] *61*

price 가격 **ga gyeok** [9-19] *25*

principal 교장 **gyo jang** [20-17] *47*

professor 교수 **gyo su** [20-10] *46*

program 프로그램 **peu ro geu raem** [26-23] *59*

pudding 푸딩 **pu ding** [35-8] *76*

pumpkin 호박 **ho bak** [38-46] *83*

pumpkin seeds 호박씨 **hobakssi** [37-30] *81*

purple 보라색 **bo ra saek** [7-8] *20*

purse 지갑 **ji gap** [9-27] *25*

put on 입다 **ib da** [8-15] *23*

Q

quarter (hour) 15분 **sip o bun** [15-7] *36*

quiet 조용한 **jo yong han** [28-10] *62*

R

rabbit 토끼 **to kki** [29-11] *64*

racket 라켓 **la kaet** [30-23] *67*

radiology 방사선과 **bang sa seon gwa** [27-33] *61*

radish 무 **mu** [38-40] *83*

railing 난간 **nan gan** [3-3] *12*

rain 비 **bi** [14-9] *34*

raincoat 비옷 **bi ot** [14-2] *34*

rainstorm 호우 **ho u** [14-27] *35*

rainwater 빗물 **bit mul** [28-26] *63*

rainy 비가오는 **biga oneun** [14-10] *34*

raise your hand 손을들다 **soneul deulda** [20-9] *46*

range hood 후드 **hu deu** [3-28] *13*

reading 읽기 **il gi** [19-2] *44*

reading a book 책 읽기 **chaek ilgi** [6-36] *18*

real 진짜 **in jja** [8-27] *23*

receipt 영수증 **yeong su jeung** [9-28] *25*

receive 받다 **bat da** [8-2] *22*

recycling 재활용 **jae hwal yong** [28-19] *63*

red 빨간색 **bbal gan saek** [7-2] *20*

red chili powder 고추가루 **gochukaroo** [38-62] *84*

red wine 적포도주 **jeok po do ju** [36-19] *79*

refrigerator 냉장고 **naeng jang go** [3-26] *13*

refund 환불 **hwanbul** [10-42] *27*

rent 월세 **weol sae** [9-29] *25*

restaurant 식당 **sik dang** [31-38] *69*

rice 밥;쌀 **bap; ssal** [34-10] *74*; [37-38] *81*

rice cake steamed over pine needles 송편 **song pyeon** [34-17] *75*

rice malt syrup 조청 **jochung** [38-73] *84*

rice porridge 죽 **juk** [34-6] *74*

rice wine 막걸리 **mak geol li** [36-23] *79*

rice wine 미린 **milin** [38-69] *84*

ride a bike 자전거를타다 **jajeongeoreul tada** [12-25] *31*

ride a train 기차를타다 **gichareul tada** [12-23] *31*

right 맞는 **mat neun** [8-26] *23*

right side 오른쪽 **oreunjjok** [13-27] *33*

river 강 **gang** [28-8] *62*

road 도로 **do ro** [11-29] *29*

rocks 바위 **ba wi** [28-20] *63*

roof 지붕 **ji bun** [3-53] *12*

room 방 **bang** [3-22] *12*; [31-21] *69*

rosemary 로즈메리 **ro jeu mae ri** [38-7] *82*

roses 장미 **jang mi** [18-14] *43*

rowing 조정 **jo jeong** [30-18] *67*

ruler 자 **ja** [19-18] *45*

running 달리기 **dal li gi** [30-9] *66*

Russian 러시아어 **Leo si a eo** [33-3] *64*

S

S size 스몰 **seu mol** [7-31] *21*

salad 샐러드 **sael leo deu** [35-13] *76*

salt 소금 **sohkeum** [38-64] *84*

sand 모래 **mo rae** [28-22] *63*

sandwich 샌드위치 **saen deu wi chi** [35-2] *76*

Santa Claus 산타크루즈 **santa keurujeu** [18-22] *43*

satisfied 만족 **man jok** [1-9] *8*

Saturday 토요일 **to yo il** [16-15] *38*

sausage 소시지 **so si ji** [35-16] *76*

savings 저축 **jeo chuk** [9-15] *25*

scallions; spring onions 파 **pa** [38-38] *83*

scarf 스카프 **seukapeu** [10-20] *27*

school 학교 **hak gyo** [20-16] *47*

school is over 하교 **ha gyo** [6-26] *18*

school uniform 교복 **gyo bok** [19-26] *45*

school vacation 학교방학 **hakgyo banghak** [18-27] *43*

science 과학 **gwa hak** [19-36] *45*; [20-12] *46*

scientist 과학자 **gwa hak ja** [25-10] *56*

scissors 가위 **ga wi** [19-22] *45*

screen 스크린 **seu keu rin** [23-2] *52*

seafood 해산물 **hae san mul** [38-11] *82*

sea water 바닷물 **ba dat mul** [31-36] *69*

season 계절 **gyae jeol** [17-18] *41*

seasonings 양념 **yangnyeom** [38-56] *84*

seaweed 김 **gim** [38-39] *83*

seaweed rice roll 김밥 **gimbap** [34-27] *75*

second 초 **cho** [15-3] *36*

secretary 비서 **bi seo** [25-17] *56*

seeds 씨앗 **ssi at** [28-24] *63*

selfie 셀피 **sael pi** [24-14] *55*

senior high school 고등학교 **go deung hak gyo** [20-29] *47*

senior year of high school 고등학교 시니어 **godeunghag-gyo sinieo** [20-32] *47*

senior year in college 대학4학년 **daehak sahaknyeon** [20-37] *47*

sentence 문장 **munjang** [21-12] *49*

September 구월 **gu wa** [16-24] *39*

sesame oil 참기름 **cham gi reum** [38-59] *84*

sesame seeds 참깨 **chamggae** [37-33] *81*

seven 일곱 **ilgop** [5-7] *16*

Seven continents of the world 세계 대륙 **saegyae chi daeryuk** [32-13] *71*

several times 여러번 **yeoleo-beon** [27-44] *61*

shake hands 악수 **ak soo** [1-28] *9*

shape 모양 **mo yang** [7-39] *21*

sheep 양 **yang** [29-15] *65*

ship; boat 배 **bae** [12-14] *31*

short 짧은 **jjalbeun** [8-5] *22*; [8-10] *22*

shirt 셔츠 **syeo cheu** [10-14] *26*

shoes 신발 **sinbal** [10-13] *26*

shop 가게 **gagae** [10-22] *27*; 상점 **sang jeom** [11-3] *28*

shop owner 가게주인 **ga gae ju in** [25-31] *57*

shop staff 점원 **jeomwon** [10-25] *27*

shopping 쇼핑 **syo ping** [11-21] *29*

shopping bag 쇼핑백 **syo-pingbaek** [10-4] *26*

short essay 짧은논문 **jjalbeunnonmun** [21-14] *49*

shoulder 어깨 **eo ggae** [4-24] *15*

shower 샤워 **sya wo gi** [3-41] *13*

shrimp; prawns 새우 **sae u** [38-14] *82*

sickness 병 **byeong** [4-48] *15*

side 옆 **yeop** [13-49] *33*

side dishes 반찬 **banchan** [34-23] *75*

sidewalk 인도 **in do** [11-27] *29*

sightseeing 관광 **gwan gwang** [31-27] *69*

silver 은색 **eun saek** [7-14] *20*

SIM card 심카드 **sim ka deu** [24-35] *54*

simple 간단 **gandan** [21-25] *49*

Singapore 싱가포르 **Sing ga po reu** [32-10] *70*

singer 가수 **ga su** [26-27] *59*

sink 싱크대 **sing keu dae** [3-40] *13*

six 여섯 **yeoseot** [5-6] *16*

six people 여섯명 **yeoseot myeong** [22-10] *51*

size 크기 **keu gi** [7-40] *21*

skiin 스키 **seu ki** [30-17] *67*

skin 피부 **pi bu** [4-41] *15*

skinny 마른 **ma reun** [8-14] *23*

skirt 치마 **chima** [10-8] *26*

sky 하늘 **ha neul** [28-23] *63*

skyscraper 고층건물 **go cheung geon mul** [11-12] *28*

slow 느린 **neu rin** [8-28] *23*

slow down 줄이다 **jul i da** [12-26] *31*

small 스몰 **seu mol** [7-37] *21*; 작은 **jak eun** [8-12] *23*

small change 잔돈 **jan don** [9-13] *25*

smaller 더 작은 **deo jakeun** [7-42] 21

smartphone 스마트폰 **seu ma teu pon** [24-1] 54

smartwatch 스마트워치 **seu ma teu weo chi** [15-14] 37

smile 미소 **mi so** [1-31] 9

snake 뱀 **baem** [29-24] 65

sneeze 재채기 **jae chae gi** [4-39] 15

snow 눈 **nun** [14-14] 34

snowball fights 눈싸움 **nun ssa um** [17-15] 41

socks 양말 **yangmal** [10-12] 26

sodas 탄산음료 **tan san eum ryo** [36-27] 79

sofa 소파 **so pa** [3-13] 12

software 소프트웨어 **so peu teu wei eo** [23-19] 53

soil 흙 **heuk** [28-21] 63

soju 소주 **so ju** [36-25] 79

solar energy 태양에너지 **taeyang aeneoji** [28-9] 62

son 아들 **a deul** [2-1] 10

song 노래 **no rae** [26-33] 59

sophomore year of high school 고등학교 2학년 **godeunghakgyo i haknyeon** [20-30] 47

sophomore year in college 대학 2학년 **daehak ihaknyeon** [20-35] 47

sound 소리 **so ri** [6-18] 18

soup 국 **kuk** [34-26] 75

south 남 **nam** [13-13] 32

South America 남아메리카 **Namamaerika** [32-15] 71

southeast 남동 **namdong** [13-12] 32

southwest 남서 **namseo** [13-11] 32

soy bean oil 콩기름 **kongireum** [38-74] 84

soy bean paste 된장 **doenjang** [38-66] 84

soy milk 두유 **du yu** [36-9] 78

soy sauce 간장 **kanjang** [38-57] 84

Spanish 서반어 **Seo ban eo** [33-6] 64

spinach 시금치 **si geum chi** [38-21] 82

spoon 숟가락 **sut ga rak** [34-15] 74

sports car 스포츠카 **seu po cheu ka** [12-10] 30

sports drinks 스포츠음료 **seu po cheu eum ryo** [36-17] 78

sports shirt; sweatshirt 운동복 **un dong bok** [30-25] 67

sports shoes; sneakers 운동화 **un dong hwa** [30-26] 67

spring 봄 **bom** [17-1] 40

stadium 경기장 **gyeong gi jang** [11-15] 29

steak 스테이크 **seu tae i keu** [35-15] 76

steamed rice cake 송편 **song pyeon** [18-16] 43

stir-fried glass noodles 잡채 **japchae** [34-25] 75

stir-fried rice cake 떡볶이 **tteokbokki** [34-22] 75

stomach 위 **wi** [4-49] 15

stopwatch 스톱워치 **seu top weo chi** [15-13] 37

stove 스토브 **seu to beu** [3-31] 13

starch 녹말 **nogmal** [38-72] 84

strawberry 딸기 **ddalgi** [37-15] 80

stream 시냇물 **si naet mul** [31-25] 69

street 거리 **geo ri** [11-4] 28

street corner 길모퉁이 **gil mo tung i** [11-30] 29

strong signal 강한신호 **ganghan sinho** [24-12] 55

story 이야기 **i ya gi** [19-32] 45

student 학생 **hak saeng** [20-15] 46

study room 공부방 **gong bu bang** [3-33] 13

study time 공부시간 **gongbu sigan** [6-35] 18

suburb 교외 **gyo wei** [11-24] 29

subway 지하철 **ji ha cheol** [12-11] 31

sugar; candy 설탕; 사탕 **seoltang; satang** [38-68] 84

summer 여름 **yeo reum** [17-2] 40

summer vacation 여름휴가 **yeoreum hyuga** [18-25] 43

sun 태양 **tae yang** [14-25] 35

sun shade 양산 **yang san** [17-10] 40

sunblock lotion 선크림 **seon keu rim** [17-16] 41

Sunday 일요일 **il yo il** [16-5] 38; [16-9] 38

sunflower seeds 해바라기씨 **haebaragissi** [37-32] 81

sunny weather 밝은날씨 **balgeun nalssi** [14-35] 35

sunny-side up eggs 한쪽덜익은계란 **hanjjok deolikeun gyaeran** [35-21] 77

supermarket 슈퍼마켓 **syu peo ma kaet** [11-5] 28

surname 성 **seong** [1-24] 9

sweater 스웨터 **seuweiteo** [14-18] 35

sweet potato 고구마 **go gu ma** [34-29] 75

swimming 수영 **su yeong** [30-19] 67

T

table 식탁 **sik tak** [3-12] 12

table lamp 테이블 램프 **taeibeul laempe** [3-34] 13

table tennis 탁구 **tak gu** [30-1] 66

tablet 테블릿 **tae beul lit** [23-3] 52

taekwondo 태권도 **taekwon-do** [30-8] 66

Tagalog 타갈로그어 **Ta gal ro geu eo** [33-17] 65

take a bus; by bus 버스타다; 버스로 **beoseutada; beoseuro** [12-20] 31

take off 벗다 **beot da** [8-15] 23

talent; ability 재능; 능력 **jae neung; neung ryeok** [19-46] 45

tall 긴 **gin** [8-5] 22

tambourine 탬버린 **taembeolin** [26-4] 58

tap water 수돗물 **su dot mul** [36-11] 78

tape 테이프 **tae i peu** [19-20] 45

tasty; delicious 맛있는 **mat it neun** [35-30] 77

tax free 면세 **myeonsae** [10-41] 27

taxi 택시 **taek si** [12-2] 30

tea 차 **cha** [36-7] 78

tear 눈물 **nun mul** [4-38] 15

tearoom 찻집 **chat jip** [31-37] 69

teacher 선생님 **seon saeng nim** [20-6] 15

technician 기술자 **gi sul ja** [25-27] 57

teeth 이 **i** [4-12] 14

telephone number 전화번호 **jeonhwa beon ho** [24-24] 54

telephone operator 전화교환원 **jeonhwa gyohwan won** [25-9] 56

television 텔레비젼 **tael lae bi jyeon** [3-9] 12

temple 사찰 **sa chal** [11-36] 29

ten 열 **yeol** [5-10] 16

tennis 테니스 **tae ni seu** [30-22] 67

test 시험 **si heom** [19-45] 45

textbook 교과서 **gyo gwa seo** [20-24] 47

texting 텍스팅 **taek seu ting** [24-27] 54

Thai 타이어 **Ta i eo** [33-15] 65

Thailand 태국 **Taeguk** [32-2] 70

the East 동 **dong** [13-45] 33

the news 뉴스 **nyu seu** [19-8] 44

the North 북 **buk** [13-48] 33

the same as 같은 **gateun** [10-31] 27

the South 남 **nam** [13-46] 33

the West 서 **seo** [13-47] 33

the year after next 후년 **hu nyeon** [16-32] 39

the year before 전년 **jeon nyeon** [16-29] 39

this year 올해 **ol hae** [16-30] 39

three 셋 **saet** [5-3] 16

three books 책세권 **chaek saegwon** [22-2] 50

three cars 차세대 **cha sae dae** [22-7] 50

three quarters 4분의3 **sabunuisam** [5-12] 16

thunder 천둥 **cheon dung** [14-12] 34

thunderstorm 폭풍우 **pok pun goo** [14-13] 34

Thursday 목요일 **mok yo il** [16-13] 38

tiger 호랑이 **ho rang i** [29-4] 64

time 시간 **si gan** [15-17] 37

tired; worn out 피곤한; 닳은 **pigonhan; dalh-eun** [27-41] 61

to add 더하기 **deohagi** [5-20] 17

to allow 허락하다 **heorakhada** [13-58] 33

to answer 답하다 **dap ha da** [19-6] 44

to answer the phone 전화를 받다 **jeonhwareul batda** [24-11] 54

to appreciate; to enjoy 감상하다; 즐기다 **gamsanghada; jeulgida** [26-19] 59

to ask 묻다 **mut da** [6-19] 18

to attend elementary school 초등학교입학 **cho deung hak gyo ip hak** [20-26] 47

to bathe 목욕하다 **mo-kyokhada** [3-48] 13

to be concerned about 걱정할것 **geogjeonghal geos** [27-48] 61

to be lost 길잃다 **gililta** [13-35] 33

to become aware of 감지하다 **gam ji ha da** [31-43] *69*

to bow 인사하다 **in sa hada** [1-33] *9*

to breathe 호흡하다 **ho heup ha da** [6-21] *18*

to bring 가져오다 **gajyeooda** [10-38] *27*

to brush teeth 이닦다 **i dak da** [6-11] *19*

to buy 사다 **sada** [10-1] *26*

to call; to be called 부르다/불리 **bureuda/bullida** [1-12] *8*

to call a taxi 택시를부르다 **taeksireul bureuda** [12-34] *31*

to catch a cold 감기걸리다 **gamgi geollida** [27-10] *60*

to catch sight of 보다 **bo da** [6-23] *18*

to chat online 온라인채팅하다 **onlain chaetinghada** [23-37] *53*

to check 수표 **su pyo** [25-22] *57*

to clean/do housework 청소하다/집안일 **cheongsohada/jipanil** [3-44] *13*

to click 클릭하다 **keullikhada** [23-29] *53*

to come across 우연히만나다 **u yeon hi man na da** [31-41] *69*

to cook; to prepare a meal 요리하다;음식을만들다 **yorihada; eumsikeul mandeulda** [6-27] *18*

to cough 기침하다 **gichimhada** [27-11] *60*

to count 세다 **saeda** [5-27] *17*

to cry 울다 **ul da** [6-1] *18*

to cycle 자전거타다 **jajeongeo tada** [30-12] *66*

to dance 춤추다 **chum chu da** [26-7] *58*

to discover 발견하는 **balgyeonhaneun** [27-46] *61*

to draw blood 피뽑다 **pi ppobda** [27-6] *60*

to divide 나누기 **nanugi** [5-17] *17*

to download 내려받다 **nae ryeo bat da** [23-30] *53*

to drill 훈련하다 **hunryeonhada** [21-29] *49*

to drink 마시다 **ma si da** [36-13] *78*

to drizzle 이슬비 **i seul bi** [17-9] *40*

to exercise 운동 **un dong** [30-6] *66*

to express (good wishes) 표현하다 **pyohyunhada** [1-37] *9*

to fall sick 병들다 **byeongdeulda** [27-13] *60*

to feel 느낌 **neukkim** [27-42] *61*

to feel reassured 안심할것 **ansimhal geos** [27-47] *61*

to find 찾다 **chat da** [31-39] *69*

to flower 개화하다 **gae hwa ha da** [17-8] *40*

to go online (인터넷)접속하다 **(inteonaet) jeopsokhada** [23-31] *53*

to go through 지나가다 **jinagada** [13-54] *33*

to graduate 졸업하다 **jol eop ha da** [20-41] *47*

to harvest 수확하다 **su hwak ha da** [17-13] *41*

to have a shower 샤워하다 **shya wo ha da** [6-28] *18*

to have dinner 저녁 먹다 **jeo nyeok meok da** [6-33] *18*

to have lunch 점심 먹다 **jeom sim meok da** [6-32] *18*

to help 돕다 **dop da** [6-16] *19*

to improve 향상하다 **hyang sang ha da** [19-49] *45*

to introduce 소개하다 **so gae hada** [1-7] *8*

to kiss 뽀뽀하다 **ppo ppo hada** [1-30] *9*

to know 알다 **al da** [1-26] *9*

to laugh 웃다 **ut da** [6-2] *18*

to learn; to study 배우다; 공부하다 **baeuda; gongbuhada** [19-3] *44*

to leave 떠나다 **ddeonada** [13-55] *33*

to listen 듣다 **deut da** [6-3] *18*

to look; see 보다 **bo da** [6-4] *18*

to major 전공하다 **jeongonghada** [20-39] *47*

to make a snowman 눈사람 만들기 **nunsaram mandeulgi** [17-12] *41*

to make a telephone call 전화를걸다 **jeonhwareul geolda** [24-10] *54*

to meet 만나다 **man nada** [1-3] *8*

to move 이사하다 **i sa ha da** [6-15] *19*

to multiply 곱하기 **gophagi** [5-18] *17*

to order 주문하다 **ju mun ha da** [34-31] *75*

to pack 짐싸다 **jim ssa da** [31-44] *69*

to pay attention to 주의하다 **ju ui ha da** [31-42] *69*

to photocopy 복사하다 **bok sa ha da** [20-8] *46*

to play 놀다 **nol da** [6-20] *18*

to play soccer 축구하다 **chukgu hada** [30-2] *66*

to practice 연습하다 **yeon seup ha da** [19-25] *45*

to prepare 준비하기 **junbihagi** [21-31] *49*

to relax 쉬다 **shwi da** [6-30] *18*

to roast; to bake 굽다 **gup da** [35-32] *77*

to scan 스캔하다 **seukaenhada** [23-11] *52*

to sell 팔다 **palda** [10-2] *26*

to send email 이메일보내다 **imaeil bonaeda** [23-39] *53*

to shop 쇼핑하다 **syopinghada** [10-3] *26*

to sign in 사인하다 **sa in ha da** [23-16] *53*

to sing 노래하다 **noraehada** [26-12] *59*

to sit 앉다 **an daò** [6-6] *18*

to sleep 자다 **ja da** [6-7] *19*

to snow 눈내리다 **nunnaerida** [14-15] *34*

to speak 연설하다 **yeon seol ha da** [6-13] *19*

to stand 서다 **seo da** [6-5] *18*

to start a conversation 대화를시작하다 **daehwareul sijakhada** [1-35] *9*

to strive 노력하다 **nolyeoghada** [21-30] *49*

to subtract 빼기 **bbaegi** [5-19] *17*

to take 가져가다 **ga jyeo ga da** [31-40] *69*

to take medicine 약먹다 **yakmeokda** [27-14] *60*

to talk 말하다 **mal ha da** [6-12] *19*

to teach 가르치다 **ga reu chi da** [20-5] *46*

to tell 말하다 **malhada** [13-53] *33*

to understand 이해하다 **ihaehada** [19-24] *45; [21-26] 49*

to wake up 일어나다 **il eo na da** [6-10] *19*

to walk the dog 개 산책하기 **gae sanchakhagi** [6-17] *19*

to wash my hair 머리 감다 **meo ri gam da** [6-29] *18*

to watch TV 티비보기 **ti bi bo gi** [6-8] *19*

to wave 흔들다 **heun deul da** [1-32] *9*

to welcome 환영하다 **hwan yong hada** [1-34] *9*

to write 쓰다 **sseu da** [6-9] *19*

toast 토스트 **to seu teu** [35-22] *77*

toaster 토스터 **to seu teo** [3-30] *13*

today 오늘 **o neul** [16-7] *38*

toenails 발톱 **bal top** [4-45] *15*

toes 발가락 **bal ga rak** [4-16] *14*

tofu 두부 **du bu** [38-42] *83*

toilet bowl 변기 **byeon gi** [3-43] *13*

tomato 토마토 **to ma to** [38-26] *83*

tomorrow 내일 **nae il** [16-8] *38*

tongue 혀 **hyeo** [4-11] *14*

topic 주제 **ju jae** [20-40] *47*

tour guide 여행안내자 **yeohaeng annaejau** [31-5] *68*

tourist 관광객 **gwan gwang gaek** [31-3] *68*

tourist attraction 여행지역 **yeohaeng jiyeok** [31-6] *68*

tourist bus 관광 버스 **gwan gwang beo seu** [31-11] *68*

town 시내 **si nae** [31-26] *69*

toys 장난감 **jangnangam** [10-18] *27*

traffic 교통 **gyo tong** [11-33] *29*

traffic lights 신호등 **sinhodeung** [11-37] *29*

train 기차 **gi cha** [12-15] *31*

train schedule 열차시간표 **yeolcha siganpyo** [12-30] *31*

train station 기차역 **gi cha yeok** [11-9] *28; [31-34] 69*

tram 전차 **jeon cha** [12-17] *31*

transfer 갈아타다 **gal a ta da** [12-35] *31*

translation 번역 **beonyeok** [21-19] *49*

travel by airplane 비행여행 **bihaeng yeohaeng** [31-8] *68*

travel by subway 지하철여행 **jihacheol yeohaeng** [31-9] *68*

tree 나무 **na mu** [28-14] *63*

trip; to travel 여행하다 **yeo haeng ha da** [31-15] *69*

trousers 바지 **baji** [10-10] *26*

truck 트럭 **teu reok** [12-5] *30*

trumpet 트럼펫 **teuleompes** [26-10] *58*

Tuesday 화요일 **hwa yo il** [16-11] *38*

turkey 칠면조 **chil myeon jo** [35-10] *76*

Turkish 터키어 **Teo ki eo** [33-7] *64*

turn left/turn right 좌회전/우회전 **jwa hwei jeon/u hwei jeon** [12-28] *31; [13-30] 33; [13-32] 33*

Twitter 트위터 **teu wi teo** [24-5] *54*

two 둘 **dul** [5-2] *16*

two; both 둘/양쪽 **dul/yangjjok** [5-22] *17*

Photo Credits

Dreamstime.com: Georgerudy *60*; Jackbluee *74*; Li Lin *35*; Natalya Aksenova *65* / **Shutterstock.com**: 54613 *74*; 89studio *45*; Africa Studio *22, 27, 37, 46, 58, 78, 82*; akepong srichaichana *81, 83*; Aleksandar Todorovic *71*; AlenKadr *74*; Alex Staroseltsev *65*; Alexander Raths *72*; ALEXEY FILATOV *52*; AlexLMX *44*; Algol *65*; Alhovik *21*; AlinaMD *35*; All kind of people *39*; all_about_people *11*; amasterphotographer *80*; AmyLv *81*; Anastasiia Skorobogatova *80*; Anatolii Riepin *76*; Andrey Burmakin *68*; Andrey Lobachev *24*; Andrey_Popov *19*; Angela Ostafichuk *42*; angelo lano *40*; Annette Shaff *14*; Anton_Ivanov *29*; antpkr *22*; Anucha Naisuntorn *36*; anueing *16*; aphotostory *37, 62*; Apple's Eyes Studio *60*; arek_malang *19*; Artem_Graf *79*; artemisphoto *43*; ArtFamily *33*; ArtOfPhotos *32*; ARTRAN *endpaper, front cover, 28, 30*; ARZTSAMUI *26*; Ase *62*; asiandelight *41*; AsiaTravel *28*; Asier Romero *8, 11, 18*; aslysun *13, 14, 18, 19, 48, 60*; Athapet Piruksa *52*; Atstock Productions *61*; Atstock Productions *61*; AV_photo *50*; AVAVA *56*; AYakovlev *58*; azure1 *81*; BalancePhoto *26*; BaLL LunLa *60*; becky's *endpaper*; Belka10 *78*; bergamont *82, 83*; Beto Chagas *67*; Bikeworldtravel *front cover*; Binh Thanh Bui *82*; Bloomicon *52*; BlueSkyImage *67*; Bo1982 *75*; Bohbeh *44*; bonchan *82*; BOONCHUAY PROMJIAM *65*; Boris Sosnovyy *22*; bright *22*; Burdun Iliya *58*; Butterfly Hunter *14*; Bychykhin Olexandr *42*; byvalet *71*; Caftor *21*; Catwalk Photos *73*; CHAjAMP *18, 37*; Chalermchai Chamnanyon *81*; chanut iamnoy *23*; charnsitr *37*; Chinaview *58*; Chones *78*; Christian Jung *80*; Chubarov Alexandr *30*; Chutima Chaochaiya *46*; Coffeemill *64*; Coprid *41*, Creativa Images *10, 19*; crystalfoto *50*; Csdesign86 *36*; cynoclub *64*; Dacian G *52*; Dark Moon Pictures *34*; Dashu *endpaper*; Dashu Xinganling *62*; DavidNNP *28*; Dean Drobot *69*; defpicture *64*; demidoff *35*; Denis Rozhnovsky *52*; DenisNata *13*; Det-anan *12*; Deyan Denchev *70*; Diego Cervo *30*; Dimasik_sh *13*; diogoppr *76*; Dmitriy Bryndin *72*; Dmitry Kalinovsky *endpaper, 48*; Dmitry Skutin *58*; dotshock *17, 67*; DoublePHOTO studio *endpaper, 31*; Dragan Milovanovic *26*; Dragon Images *19, 44, 56, 60, 66*; dugdax *63*; DVARG *52*; dwphotos *66*; eAlisa *51*; East *18*; Eastfenceimage *11*; Eatmann *58*; Ebtikar *32*; effective stock photos *64*; Egor Rodynchenko *80*; Ekkamai Chaikanta *78*; Elena Elisseeva *78*; Elena Schweitzer *80*; Elena Vasilchenko *60*; Elina-Lava *73*; Elnur *26, 72*; elwynn *15, 18, 26*; Enlightened Media *81*; EQRoy *28*; Eric Isselee *23, 64, 65*; ESB Professional *21, 33, 35, 46*; Etaphop photo *77*; Eugene Onischenko *66*; Evan Lorne *55*; Evangelos *30*; Evgenyi *83*; Fazakas Mihaly *50*; fear1ess *55*; FeellFree *80*; feelplus *33*; Ferenc Szelepcsenyi *59*; fizkes *62*; Food1.it *76*; fotohunter *endpaper, 40*; Fototaras *40*; Francesco83 *16*; Frank Fiedler *20*; Freedom_Studio *33*; furtseff *58*; Gallinago_media *65*; George Dolgikh *20, 76, 79*; GMEVIPHOTO *77*; Gnilenkov Aleksey *35*; Goga Shutter *31*; gogoiso *26*; Goodmorning3am *62*; GooDween123 *34*; gowithstock *endpaper, 78*; Green Jo *40*; gresei *77*; Grigor Unkovski *84*; Grobler du Preez *65*; Guitar photographer *42*; Gumpanat *25*; Guzel Studio *71*; Halfbottle *32, 57*; Hallgerd *34*; Hans Kim *front cover, 32, 52, 57*; HelloRF Zcool *46*; HGalina *32*; HomeStudio *7*; Hong Vo *81*; Howard Sandler *73*; humphery *55*; Hung Chung Chih *71*; Hurst Photo *67*; hxdbzxy *46*; hxdyl *74*; I'm friday *30*; Iakov Filimonov *25, 32*; iamlukyeee *42*; iaodesign *76*; IB Photography *52, 55*; ifong *22, 30*; Igor Bulgarin *59*; Igor Plotnikov *70*; Igor Sh *78*; Igors Rusakovs *82*; iko *14*; imtmphoto *9, 11*; inbevel *41*; IndigoLT *72*; Inna Astakhova *65*; interstid *8*; iofoto *10*; irin-k *27, 65*; Ivan Demyanov *22*; Ivan Smuk *67*; Jackbluee *74*; Jakkrit Orrasri *84*; Jane0606 *55*; jaroslava V *64*; jazz3311 *79*; Jeanne McRight *57*; JEONGHYEON NOH *front flap*; jianbing Lee *44*; JIANG HONGYAN *82, 83*; Jiang Zhongyan *84*; Jiri Hera *84*; joesayhello *75*; John Bill *41*; jreika *75*; Juan Ci *49*; Kamenetskiy Konstantin *9, 66*; Karkas *25*; Karramba Production *67*; Kate Aedon *19*; kathayut kongmanee *42*; Kaveex *62*; kazoka *41*; Kazuki Nakagawa *34*; kc look *endpaper*; kedrov *26*; Keith Homan *endpaper, 78, 79*; kellyreekolibry *83*; Khomulo Anna *68*; Kim JinKwon *back cover, 73*; Kirill Vorobyev *65*; KITSANANAN *81*; KK Tan *56*; Kletr *65*; Kokhanchikov *76*; komkrich ratchusiri *front cover*; Kongsak *74*; Konstantin Zubarev *26, 27*; KPG Ivary *37*; KPG_Mega *back cover, 42*; KPG_Payless *34*; Ksander *52*; kudla *68*; Kzenon *23, 29, 43*; LazyFocus *65*; LDWYTN *56*; Lemberg Vector studio *54*; leolintang *73*; Leonid Ikan *40*; leungchopan *8, 11, 55, 56, 57, 68*; Lev Kropotov *63*; LifetimeStock *72*; Lisy *79*; livingpitty *37*; Ljupco Smokovski *63*; Lonely *34*; Lotus Images *43, 83*; Lunghammer *66*; M. Unal Ozmen *76*; M.Stasy *44*; Macrovector *13*; Madlen *81*; Maks Narodenko *80, 81*; Marcos Mesa Sam Wordley *21*; margouillat photo *76*; Maridav *40, 67*; Mariusz Szczygiel *78*; maroke *8, 57*; martinho Smart *12*; Matej Kastelic *68*; Maxim Tupikov *67*; maximmmmum *42*; Maxx-Studio *68*; michaeljung *68, 72*; Michiel de Wit *64*; MidoSemsem *80*; Milkovasa *68*; Milles Studio *43*; Ministr-84 *30*; mirana *53*; miya227 *8, 25*; Monkey Business Images *9, 10, 11, 12, 19, 44, 56*; monticello *76, 77*; mountainpix *73*; mphot *59*; MSSA *15*; Myibean *80*; Nagy-Bagoly Arpad *59*; naka-stockphoto *9*; Namart Pieamsuwan *45*; Natalia D. *65*; Nattika *80*; natu *11*; Nawanon *66*; Nerthuz *31, 62*; Nghia Khanh *29, 71*; Nicole Kwiatkowski *71*; nik7ch *12*; Nikita Rogul *29*; Nikki Zalewski *20*; Nikolas_jkd *36*; NIPAPORN PANYACHAROEN *83*; NoonBuSin *endpaper*; norikko *front cover, endpaper, 75*; npine *75*; ntstudio *80*; nui7711 *55*; Nuk2013 *77*; number-one *19, 72*; NYS *26*; oatawa *37*; odd-add *40*; Odua Images *37, 38, 74*; Oksana Mizina *81*; oksana2010 *65*; Oleksandr Yuhlchek *53*; Oleksandra Naumenko *77*; Olesia Bilkei *35*; Olga Kashubin *71*; Ollinka *35*; onair *80*; OPOLJA *51*; optimarc *50, 82, 83*; ostill *62, 67*; OZaiachin *58*; Palis Michalis *52*; panda3800 *80*; pathdoc *32*; Patrick Foto *70*; Patrick Krabeepetcharat *74*; paulaphoto *10*; pcruciatti *54*; Pepsco Studio *54*; Peter Hermes Furian *61*; phive *84*; photka *45*; photo5963_shutter *23*; Photographee.eu *13, 56*; photomaster *65*; PhotoRoman *70*; photosync *65*; Phovoir *72*; Picsfive *78, 80*; pinunpa *77*; pio3 *67*; Pixel Embargo *25*; pnsam *75*; PORTRAIT IMAGES ASIA BY NONWARIT *18*; ppart *24*; PR Image Factory *13*; Praisaeng *73*; Prasit Rodphan *46*; Pressmaster *42, 66*; Preto Perola *44*; PrinceOfLove *56, 78*; ProfStocker *41*; pryzmat *25*; PSboom *70*; PT Images *11*; racorn *46*; rangizzz *80*; ratmaner *35*; Rawpixel.com *30, 43, 50, 56, 63, 68, 74*; redstrap *31*; Rido *74*; risteski goce *31*; Rob Wilson *28*; Roman.Volkow *37*; Romaset *60*; RossHelen *26*; RPBaiao *70*; RTimages *36*; Rudchenko Liliia *82*; rvlsoft *54*; Ryszard Stelmachowicz *35*; S-F *65*; Sagase48 *68*; saiko3p *80*; Sanga Park *endpaper*; Santibhavank P *60*; Sathit *76*; sattahipbeach *25*; Scanrail1 *44, 78*; ScriptX *77*; Sean Heatley *70*; Sean Locke Photography *38*; Sean Pavone *70*; sergo1972 *50*; Settawat Udom *71*; sezer66 *63*; Shanti Hesse *68*; She *50*; shopplaywood *32*; Shumo4ka *20*; Silvy78 *81*; Sinseeho *14*; skyfish *40*; Smileus *40*; sociologas *20*; Solomatina Julia *20*; SOMMAI *82*; Son Hoang Tran *59*; sonnim *29*; Sonya illustration *20*; Sorbis *28, 77*; Spacedromedary *25*; spaxiax *76*; spiber.de *44*; Spotmatik Ltd *60*; ssuaphotos *62*; Stanisic Vladimir *54*; Stanislav Khokholkov *72*; steamroller_blues *79*; stockphoto mania *28*; stockphoto-graf *79*; Stone36 *35*; Stuart Jenner *8, 19, 56, 80*; Studio KIWI *84*; studioloco *41*; successo images *back cover, 74, 75*; SUNG YOON JO *55*; swissmacky *32*; Syda Productions *68*; Sylvie Bouchard *54*; szefei *11, 44, 66, 73*; tab62 *11*; takayuki *10, 19*; tanuha2001 *54, 78*; Tanya Sid *76*; taveesak srisomthavil *40*; Teguh Mujiono *15*; TENGLAO *73*; testing *30, 66*; Thanit Weerawan *79*; Thanthima Lim *endpaper, 84*; The Len *41*; theerasakj *11*; themorningglory *81*; Tim UR *81*; timquo *81*; TK Kurikawa *28, 29, 30, 31*; TMON *74, 75*; Tobik *82*; Tom Wang *8, 14, 34, 42, 44, 47, 57, 62*; Tony Magdaraog *73*; Top Photo Engineer *front cover, 66*; topseller *43*; TRINACRIA PHOTO *45*; Tsekhmister *64*; TTstudio *63*; twentyfour-seven *spine, endpaper, 58*; ucchie79 *11*; Valdis Skudre *34*; Valentina Razumova *76*; Valentyn Volkov *76, 80*; vandycan *27*; vectorshape *53*; Veronica Louro *30*; vhpfoto *34*; Viktoria Gaman *42*; vipman *13*; Visaro *29*; visivastudio *22*; vitals *81*; Vitaly Korovin *17*; Vlad Teodor *26*; Vladimir Wrangel *64*; Vladislav S º*81*; Volosina *84*; wacpan *43*; Wallenrock *78*; wavebreakmedia *22, 56, 59*; WDG Photo *62*; withGod *51*; wizdata *endpaper, 42*; wong yu liang *57*; xmee *70*; YanLev *43*; Yeongsik Im *endpaper*; Yingha *75*; Yuri Samsonov *78*; Zacarias Pereira da Mata *35*; zcw *79*; zeljkodan *43*; Zerbor *61*; zhu difeng *28*; ZinaidaSopina *28*; Zush *83*

Published by Tuttle Publishing, an imprint of Periplus Editions (HK) Ltd

www.tuttlepublishing.com

ISBN: 978-0-8048-4932-6

24 23 22   10 9 8 7
Printed in Malaysia   2206TO

"Books to Span the East and West"

Tuttle Publishing was founded in 1832 in the small New England town of Rutland, Vermont [USA]. Our core values remain as strong today as they were then—to publish best-in-class books which bring people together one page at a time. In 1948, we established a publishing office in Japan—and Tuttle is now a leader in publishing English-language books about the arts, languages and cultures of Asia. The world has become a much smaller place today and Asia's economic and cultural influence has grown. Yet the need for meaningful dialogue and information about this diverse region has never been greater. Over the past seven decades, Tuttle has published thousands of books on subjects ranging from martial arts and paper crafts to language learning and literature—and our talented authors, illustrators, designers and photographers have won many prestigious awards. We welcome you to explore the wealth of information available on Asia at **www.tuttlepublishing.com**.

Distributed by

North America, Latin America & Europe
Tuttle Publishing
364 Innovation Drive
North Clarendon,
VT 05759-9436 U.S.A.
Tel: 1 (802) 773-8930
Fax: 1 (802) 773-6993
info@tuttlepublishing.com
www.tuttlepublishing.com

Japan
Tuttle Publishing
Yaekari Building, 3rd Floor
5-4-12 Osaki
Shinagawa-ku
Tokyo 141-0032
Tel: (81) 3 5437-0171
Fax: (81) 3 5437-0755
sales@tuttle.co.jp
www.tuttle.co.jp

Asia Pacific
Berkeley Books Pte. Ltd.
3 Kallang Sector, #04-01/02,
Singapore 349278
Tel: (65) 67412178
Fax: (65) 67412179
inquiries@periplus.com.sg
www.tuttlepublishing.com

How to Download the Online Audio of this Book.

1. Make sure you have an Internet connection.

2. Type the URL below into your web browser.

http://www.tuttlepublishing.com/korean-picture-dictionary-downloadable-content

For support, you can email us at info@tuttlepublishing.com.

복숭아꽃
bok sung a ggot
peach blossoms

음력 새해
eumryeok saehae
Lunar New Year

숟가락
sut ga rak
spoon

젓가락
jeot ga rak
chopsticks

서법
seo beop
calligraphy

북
buk
drum

경복궁
Gyeongbokgung
Gyeongbokgung
Palace